The *Children's* Baking Book

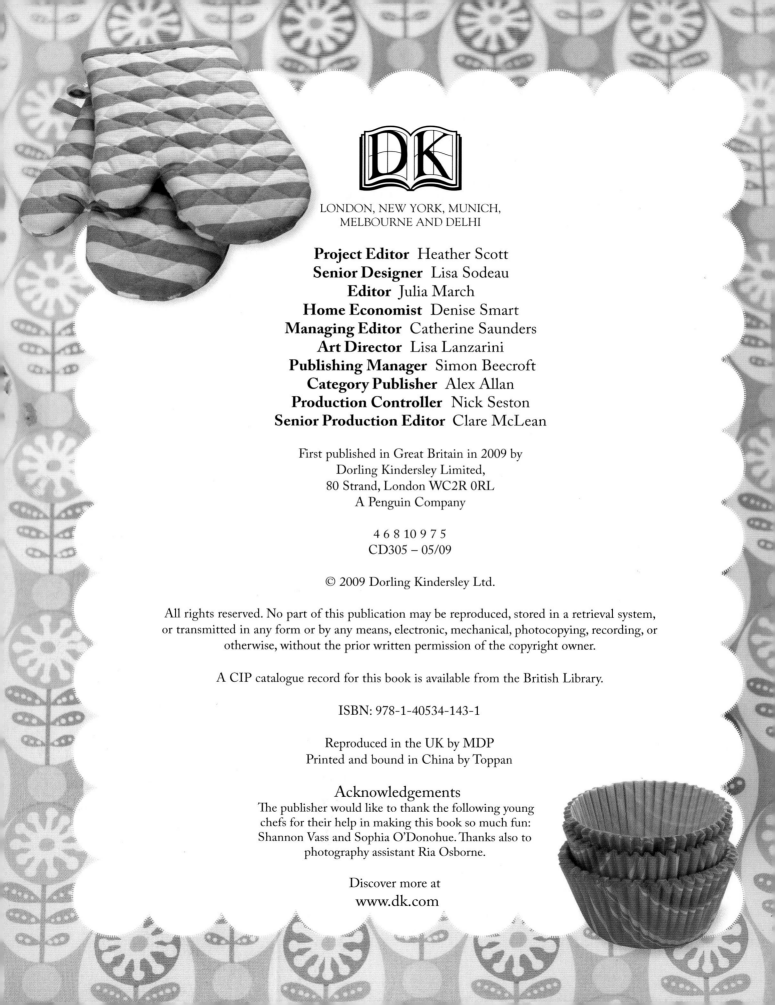

DK

LONDON, NEW YORK, MUNICH,
MELBOURNE AND DELHI

Project Editor Heather Scott
Senior Designer Lisa Sodeau
Editor Julia March
Home Economist Denise Smart
Managing Editor Catherine Saunders
Art Director Lisa Lanzarini
Publishing Manager Simon Beecroft
Category Publisher Alex Allan
Production Controller Nick Seston
Senior Production Editor Clare McLean

First published in Great Britain in 2009 by
Dorling Kindersley Limited,
80 Strand, London WC2R 0RL
A Penguin Company

4 6 8 10 9 7 5
CD305 – 05/09

A CIP catalogue record for this book is available from the British Library.

ISBN: 978-1-40534-143-1

Reproduced in the UK by MDP
Printed and bound in China by Toppan

Acknowledgements
The publisher would like to thank the following young
chefs for their help in making this book so much fun:
Shannon Vass and Sophia O'Donohue. Thanks also to
photography assistant Ria Osborne.

Discover more at
www.dk.com

Recipes & Styling by Denise Smart
Photography by Howard Shooter

Contents

page 54

 Introduction 6-7

Biscuits, Cookies and Traybakes 8-9

page 30

page 40

Sticky Toffee Squares	10-11
Chocolate and Cranberry Cookies	12-13
Cheesy Shortbread	14-15
Chocolate Fridge Squares	16-17
Rocky Road Cookies	18-19
Raisin Biscuits	20-21
Melting Moments	22-23
Jam Shapes	24-25
Cheesy Oatcakes	26-27
Orange and Seed Cookies	28-29
Star Biscuits	30-31
Flapjacks	32-33
Ginger and Pumpkin Slices	34-35
Coconut Biscuits	36-37
Chocolate Fudge Brownies	38-39
Gingerbread	40-41

Doughs 42-43

Basic Bread	44-45
Scones	46-47
Cheese and Onion Round	48-49
Pizza Dough	50-51
Multi-Grain Plait	52-53
Sticky Fruit Buns	54-55
Italian Bread	56-57
Cornbread	58-59
Flatbreads	60-61

page 44

page 76

page 96

page 112

Cakes 62-63

Simple Sponge Cake	64-65
Double Chocolate Fudge Cake	66-67
Carrot Cupcakes	68-69
Banana and Buttermilk Cake	70-71
Marble Cake	72-73
Lemon Drizzle Cake	74-75
Savoury Muffins	76-77
Blueberry and Sour Cream Cake	78-79
Cake Roll	80-81
Orange and Poppy Seed Muffins	82-83
Tropical Fruit Cake	84-85
Lime and Coconut Cupcakes	86-87
Oat and Honey Muffins	88-89
Cocoa Mint Meringues	90-91
Upside-down Apple Cake	92-93
Mini Muffins	94-95
Baked Raspberry Cheesecake	96-97

Pastry 98-99

Chocolate Profiterôles	100-101
Cherry and Berry Pie	102-103
Chocolate Tart	104-105
Lemon Meringue	106-107
Banoffee Pie	108-109
Chicken and Ham Pies	110-111
Tomato and Basil Tart	112-113
Filo and Spinach Tarts	114-115
Strawberry Tartlets	116-117
Apple Crumble	118-119
Bacon and Egg Tart	120-121

page 116

page 94

★ Decoration 122-123

★ Glossary 124-125

★ Index 126-128

Introduction

It is so satisfying to eat food you have cooked yourself, and baking is one of the most enjoyable methods of cooking. Baking uses lots of great techniques and delicious ingredients, and best of all, it fills your kitchen with the most wonderful smells!

Safe baking

Baking is great fun, but with heat and sharp objects around you must always take care to be safe and sensible.

- Use oven gloves when handling hot pans, trays or bowls.
- Don't put hot pans or trays directly onto the work surface – use a heatproof trivet, mat, rack or board.
- When you are stirring food on the cooker, grip the handle firmly to steady the pan.
- When cooking on the hob, turn the pan handles to the side (away from the heat and the front) so that you are less likely to knock them over.
- Take extra care on any step where you see the warning triangle symbol.

Getting started

1. Read the recipe through before you begin.
2. Wash your hands, tie your hair back (if necessary) and put on an apron.
3. Gather all the ingredients and equipment you need.
4. Start baking!

How to use the spreads

There's a lot of information packed onto each page, so here's how to get the best out of the recipes. You'll find simple instructions, tips, delicious variations and mouthwatering recipes.

The lists of tools and ingredients tell you everything you will need.

The introduction tells you a bit about the recipe.

This tells you the level of difficulty and the colour indicates which section of the book the recipe is in.

Check here for how many the recipe makes or serves and how long it will take.

The chef's tip will give you some useful cooking advice.

Step-by-step pictures and text will guide you through the recipes.

Many of the recipes can be adapted to make different flavours.

Kitchen hygiene

After safety, cleanliness is the most important thing to be aware of in the kitchen. Here are a few simple hygiene rules for you to follow:

- Always wash your hands before you start baking, and after handling raw meat.
- Wash all fruit and vegetables.
- Use separate chopping boards for meat and vegetables.
- Keep your cooking area clean and have a cloth handy to wipe up any spills.
- Store cooked and raw food separately.
- Always check the use-by date on all ingredients. Do not use them if the date has passed.
- Keep meat in the refrigerator until you need it and always take care to cook it thoroughly.

Biscuits, Cookies and Traybakes

In this section there are lots of delicious recipes for individual baked treats. Biscuits, cookies and traybakes are quite easy to make and because they often don't need long to cook, they are perfect for a quick baking session.

Mixing

Mixing means putting ingredients together. You can do this by hand, or with a spoon, hand whisk, electric whisk or food processor.

Top Tip

When you are cutting out shapes for biscuits, cut out as many as you can and then gather up the scraps and roll them out again. Repeat until you have used up all the dough and none is wasted.

Rolling and cutting out

When rolling out dough with a rolling pin, make sure the work surface and the rolling pin are sprinkled with flour to prevent the dough from sticking. When cutting out, gently wiggle the cutter from side to side – you will find it lifts out easily.

Top Tip

Always use unsalted butter unless the recipe tells you otherwise. Salted butter burns more easily and is less healthy.

Measuring

Measuring out ingredients is important. The ingredients in these recipes have been carefully calculated so that the finished baked foods turn out just right. The amounts needed are given in metric and imperial measurements. Always stick to one version.

Storage

If you have any leftovers or want to save your creations for later, put them in a sealed, airtight container to keep them fresh.

Easy

Makes
24

Prep
10
mins

Cooking
30
mins

Toffee Squares

These toffee squares are yummy! For extra stickiness the squares are topped with a caramel toffee sauce. You can buy this in a jar but it's more fun to make your own.

Palette knife

Flour

Eggs

Ingredients

- 150g (5oz) pitted soft dates (roughly chopped)
- 125ml (4floz) cold water
- 1tsp bicarbonate of soda
- 150g (5oz) butter (softened)
- 150g (5oz) light muscovado sugar
- 2 medium eggs (beaten)
- 1tsp vanilla extract
- 175g (6oz) self-raising flour

Toffee topping
- 6tbsp caramel toffee sauce (Dulce de Leche)

Tools

- 28cm x 18cm (11"x 7") tin
- Baking paper
- Small saucepan
- Large mixing bowl
- Electric or hand whisk
- Metal spoon
- Oven gloves
- Cooling rack
- Chopping board
- Sharp knife
- Palette knife

Saucepan

Sugar

Dates

Chef's Tip
These cakes taste delicious served warm drizzled with caramel sauce and cream or ice cream.

1 Preheat the oven to 180°C (350°F, gas mark 4). Lightly grease a 28cm x 18cm (11" x 7") tin and line the base with baking paper to prevent the cake from sticking.

2 Place the dates in a pan and add the water. Bring to the boil, then remove from the heat and add the bicarbonate of soda – the mixture will fizz! Leave to one side to cool slightly.

3 Place the butter and sugar in a large mixing bowl. Using an electric or hand whisk, beat them together until they are light and fluffy. Whisk in the eggs and vanilla extract.

4 Using a metal spoon fold in the flour, then the date mixture. Pour the mixture into the tin. Place it in the centre of the oven and cook for 25–30 minutes, or until risen.

5 Allow the cake to cool in the tin for 10 minutes, then transfer it to a cooling rack. When cold, cut it into 24 squares, then spread your caramel sauce over the top with a palette knife.

Chef's Tip

To make your own caramel sauce, bring 75g (3oz) butter, 150g (5oz) light brown soft sugar and 150ml (¼pt) single cream to the boil and cook for 3 minutes, until thickened. Allow to cool.

Chocolate and Cranberry Cookie

The perfect combination of bitter cranberries and sweet white chocolate makes these cookies melt in your mouth!

Chef's Tip

Eat these moreish cookies while they are still warm – as the chocolate will be gooey. Delicious!

Tools

- Two baking sheets
- Baking paper
- Large mixing bowl
- Electric or hand whisk
- Dessert spoon
- Oven gloves
- Cooling rack
- Flipper

Large mixing bowl

Ingredients

Sugar

Butter

- 125g (4oz) butter (softened)
- 125g (4oz) soft light brown sugar
- 1 medium egg (beaten)
- 1tbsp milk
- 150g (5oz) plain flour
- ½tsp baking powder
- 50g (2oz) white chocolate (finely grated)
- 100g (3½oz) white chocolate chips
- 50g (2oz) dried cranberries

 Plain flour

Dried cranberries

Milk

1 Preheat the oven to 180°C (375°F, gas mark 4). Line two baking sheets with baking paper to prevent the cookies from sticking while they are baking.

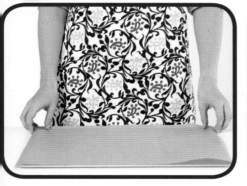

2 Cream the butter and sugar together in a large bowl until they are pale and creamy. (You can use a hand or electric whisk.) Then beat in the egg and milk with the whisk.

3 Add the flour, baking powder, grated chocolate, chocolate chips and cranberries to the mixture. Using a dessert spoon, stir until they are thoroughly mixed together.

4 Place dessert spoonfuls of the cookie mixture onto the prepared baking sheets. Leave space between the spoonfuls so the cookies do not merge together as they cook.

5 Bake for 12–15 minutes, until lightly golden and slightly soft to the touch. Allow to cool on the sheet for 5 minutes, then transfer to a cooling rack to cool completely.

Variation

Milk or plain chocolate would also taste great in these cookies. If you prefer other dried fruits such as strawberries or blueberries, use them instead of cranberries.

Cheesy Shortbread

These light and buttery savoury cheese biscuits make a perfect afternoon snack. Or serve them at a party and watch them disappear!

Chef's Tip

Freshly grated Parmesan gives the best flavour, but dried Parmesan can also be used.

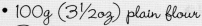
Plain flour

Ingredients

Egg yolk

- 100g (3½oz) plain flour
- Pinch of cayenne pepper
- 100g (3½oz) butter (diced)
- 75g (3oz) Parmesan cheese (freshly grated)
- 1 egg yolk
- 1tsp olive oil

To glaze
- Egg yolk beaten with a little milk
- 1tsp poppy seeds

Cookie cutter

Tools

- Large baking sheet
- Large mixing bowl
- Metal spoon
- Round-bladed knife
- Cling film
- Rolling pin
- 5cm (2") round cookie cutter
- Pastry brush
- Oven gloves
- Palette knife
- Cooling rack

Baking tray

1 Lightly grease a large baking sheet with butter. Preheat the oven to 170°C (325°F, gas mark 3). Place the flour and cayenne pepper in a large mixing bowl and mix together with a metal spoon.

2 Add the butter to the flour mixture. Rub it in using your fingertips until the mixture resembles breadcrumbs. Then stir in the Parmesan cheese with a metal spoon.

Butter

Olive oil

3 Add the egg yolk and olive oil and stir the mixture together with a round-bladed knife. Using your hands, form the mixture into a ball of dough. Wrap it in cling film and chill for 30 minutes.

4 Using a floured rolling pin, roll out the chilled dough on a lightly floured surface to 5mm (½") thick. Using a 5cm (2") round cutter, cut out 16 circles. Put them on the baking sheet.

5 Brush the tops of the circles with the egg yolk glaze and then sprinkle them with the poppy seeds. Bake them on the top shelf for 20–25 minutes, or until golden.

6 Leave the shortbread biscuits to cool on the baking sheet for a few minutes. Then, using a palette knife, transfer them to a cooling rack to cool completely.

Chocolate Fridge Squares

These crunchy chocolate fruit and nut squares couldn't be easier to make – they don't even need cooking!

Makes
18

Prep
15 mins

Setting
2 hours

Saucepan

Tools

- 18cm x 28cm (11" x 7") cake tin
- Baking paper
- Saucepan
- Wooden spoon
- Large mixing bowl
- Blunt knife
- Chopping board

Chocolate

Dried apricots

Ingredients

- 200g (7oz) 70% cocoa plain chocolate (broken into pieces)
- 100g (3½oz) butter (diced)
- 4tbsp golden syrup
- 225g (8oz) digestive biscuits (broken into pieces)
- 125g (4oz) whole shelled pistachios
- 200g (7oz) dried apricots (roughly chopped)
- 100g (3½oz) dried cranberries or cherries

Wooden spoon

Golden syrup

Butter

Dried cranberries

Chef's Tip

For a citrus twist, add the grated zest of an orange to the chocolate, butter and golden syrup mixture.

1 Line a 18cm x 28cm (11" x 7") tin with baking paper. Place the chocolate, butter and golden syrup in a saucepan over a low heat. Stir occasionally until they are melted and smooth.

2 Place all the remaining ingredients in a large mixing bowl and mix well. Pour over the chocolate mixture and stir until all the ingredients are evenly coated.

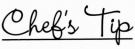

3 Tip the mixture into the prepared tin and spread it evenly with the back of a spoon. Chill for at least 2 hours or until firm to the touch.

4 Run a blunt knife around the edge of the tin. Carefully turn out onto a chopping board and remove the baking paper. Cut the fridge cake into squares and serve.

Variation

You can replace the dried cranberries or cherries with the same quantity of currants, raisins, glacé cherries or prunes.

Rocky Road Cookies

These gorgeous cookies are topped with chunky chocolate and melted marshmallows. The chunky and smooth textures are a perfect combination – yum!

Tools

- Two baking sheets
- Baking paper
- Large mixing bowl
- Electric or hand whisk
- Metal spoon
- Dessert spoon
- Oven gloves
- Palette knife
- Cooling rack

Palette knife

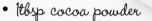
Chocolate

Brown sugar

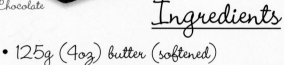

Ingredients

- 125g (4oz) butter (softened)
- 125g (4oz) soft brown sugar
- 1 medium egg (beaten)
- 1 tbsp milk
- 50g (2oz) milk chocolate (chopped)
- 125g (4oz) plain flour

- 1tbsp cocoa powder
- ½tsp baking powder
- 50g (2oz) white chocolate (chopped)
- 25g (1oz) mini marshmallows

Large mixing bowl

Plain flour

Egg

1 Preheat the oven to 180°C (375°F, gas mark 4). Line two baking sheets with baking paper. Use an electric or hand whisk to cream the butter and sugar together in a mixing bowl.

2 Beat in the egg and milk. Then stir in the flour, cocoa powder, baking powder and half the chunks of milk and white chocolate using a metal spoon.

3 Place dessert spoons of the mixture onto the prepared baking sheets, spacing them well apart. Flatten slightly and bake for 5 minutes, until the edges are starting to get firm.

4 Remove the cookies from the oven. Immediately sprinkle them with the marshmallows and remaining chocolate chunks, pressing them down into the cookies.

5 Return the cookies to the oven for a further 5–6 minutes or until slightly soft to the touch. Allow them to cool for 5 minutes, then transfer them to a cooling rack.

Variation

Experiment with different flavoured chocolate chunks. Or try heart-shaped marshmallows for a Valentine's Day treat!

Raisin Biscuits

These simply scrumptious biscuits are sure to become a favourite. They are perfect for an afternoon snack or a light dessert.

Makes

20

Prep

20 mins

Cooking

14 mins

Variation

Replace the raisins with currants if you prefer them or spice things up by adding a little cinnamon or mixed spice.

Ingredients

Butter

Egg

Lemon

- 125g (4oz) butter (softened)
- 75g (3oz) caster sugar
- Finely grated zest of 1 lemon
- 1 egg (separated)
- 200g (7oz) plain flour (sifted)
- 75g (3oz) raisins
- 2tbsp milk
- 1–2tbsp caster sugar (for sprinkling)

Raisins

Electric whisk

Tools

Pastry brush

- Two large baking sheets
- Large mixing bowl
- Electric or hand whisk
- Round-bladed knife
- Rolling pin
- 6cm (2.5") round fluted cutter
- Oven gloves
- Fork
- Pastry brush
- Palette knife
- Cooling rack

1 Preheat the oven to 180°C (350°F, gas mark 4). Grease two baking sheets. In a bowl, beat the butter, sugar and lemon zest together using an electric or hand whisk, until they are pale and fluffy.

2 Beat in the egg yolk but keep the egg white to one side. Using a round-bladed knife, gently stir in the sifted flour and raisins. Gradually stir in the milk until the dough comes together.

3 Tip the dough onto a lightly floured surface and knead it gently until it is smooth and supple. Shape the dough into a ball with your hands.

4 Roll the dough out to about 5mm (¼") thick then cut out the biscuits using a 6cm (2.5") round fluted cutter. Place the biscuits on the baking sheets and bake for 8–10 minutes.

5 Using oven gloves, remove the baking sheets from the oven. Lightly whisk the egg white with a fork, then brush it over the biscuits with a pastry brush and sprinkle them with caster sugar.

6 Wearing the oven gloves, return the biscuits to the oven for 3–4 minutes until they turn golden. Once cooked, remove the biscuits from the oven and transfer them to a cooling rack.

Melting Moments

Makes
15

Prep
20
mins

Cooking
15
mins

These melt-in-the-mouth biscuits are a chocolate-lover's dream! The creamy filling and crunchy biscuit is a tasty combination.

Tools

- Two large baking sheets
- Baking paper
- Large mixing bowl
- Electric whisk or wooden spoon
- Sieve
- Metal spoon
- Teaspoon
- Oven gloves
- Cooling rack
- Palette knife
- Heatproof bowl
- Small saucepan
- Wooden spoon

Heatproof bowl

Butter

Ingredients

- 175g (6oz) butter (softened)
- 50g (2oz) caster sugar
- 1tsp vanilla extract
- 125g (4oz) plain flour
- 25g (1oz) cornflour
- 25g (1oz) cocoa powder (sifted)

For the filling
- 100g (3½oz) good quality chocolate (broken into pieces)
- 2tbsp double cream

Baking sheet

Sugar

Plain

Chocolate

1 Preheat the oven to 180°C (350°F, gas mark 4). Line two baking sheets with baking paper. Place the butter, sugar and vanilla extract in a bowl and beat with a whisk or wooden spoon.

2 Sift the plain flour, cornflour and cocoa powder into the mixing bowl. Using a metal spoon, fold them into the mixture until the ingredients are well combined.

3 Using a teaspoon, spoon 15 x 2.5cm (1") dollops onto each baking sheet so that you have 30 in total. Allow room between each one as they will spread whilst cooking.

Chef's Tip

For a perfect professional finish, use a piping bag with a star-shaped nozzle in Step 3. See page 123 for tips on how to make your own piping bag.

4 Bake for 12–15 minutes, or until they are just starting to become dark around the edges. Remove them from the oven and leave to cool slightly before moving to a cooling rack.

5 Place the chocolate and cream in a heatproof bowl over a saucepan of simmering water. Stir them until they have melted. Remove from the heat and leave to cool completely.

6 Spread the filling on the flat side of half of the cooled biscuits with a palette knife and sandwich each one with one of the remaining biscuits.

Jam Shapes

These pretty jam-filled biscuits take time to make, but they are definitely worth the effort! The combination of gooey jam and crunchy biscuit is heavenly.

1 Preheat the oven to 170°C (325°F, gas mark 3). Line two baking sheets with baking paper. Process the butter, sugar, vanilla extract and lemon zest in a food processor until smooth.

2 Add the egg, egg yolk and flour to the food processor and process again until the mixture resembles breadcrumbs and is starting to come together in a dough.

3 Transfer the dough to a lightly floured surface and lightly knead until it is smooth. Flatten into a circle, wrap it in cling film and chill for 30 minutes.

Ingredients

Eggs

Sugar

Food processor

- 175g (6oz) butter (softened)
- 175g (6oz) caster sugar
- 1tsp vanilla extract
- 1tsp finely grated lemon zest
- 1 medium egg (beaten)
- 1 egg yolk
- 275g (10oz) plain flour, plus a little extra for rolling out
- 6tbsp raspberry or strawberry jam
- 2tbsp icing sugar (for dusting)

Lemon

Butter

Oven gloves

Tools

Rolling pin

- Two large baking sheets
- Baking paper
- Food processor
- Cling film
- Rolling pin
- 6cm (2½") cookie cutter
- 2–3cm (1–1½") cookie cutter
- Oven gloves
- Cooling rack
- Palette knife

Chef's Tip

Use different shaped cutters for different shaped biscuits. Make sure that any cutter that you use has a smaller version to cut the hole out of the middle.

4 On a lightly floured surface, roll the dough out to 3mm (¼") thick. Using a 6cm (2½") cookie cutter, cut out as many biscuits as you can. You should get about 36 in total.

5 Use a 2–3cm (1–1½") cookie cutter to cut out the middle from 18 of the biscuits (you can bake these too if you like). Arrange on the baking sheets and chill for 15 minutes.

6 Bake on the middle shelf of the oven (in batches, if necessary) for about 10–12 minutes or until golden. Cool on the baking sheets for 1 minute, then transfer them to a cooling rack.

7 When completely cool, spread the whole biscuits with jam. Then dust icing sugar on the biscuits with holes in. Press one sugar-dusted biscuit onto each jam-covered one and serve.

Variation

You can use any flavour of jam you prefer instead of raspberry or strawberry. Try apricot or blackcurrant jam.

Cheesy Oatcakes

These crunchy savoury biscuits are delicious served warm or cold. They are perfect for a snack or a light lunch. Serve them with your favourite cheese and some salad or relish.

Variation

If you don't like rosemary just leave it out. Alternatively, you could add 1tsp dried mixed herbs.

Egg yolk

Cheese

Oven gloves

Rolling pin

Ingredients

- 225g (8oz) medium oatmeal
- 50g (2oz) Cheddar cheese (finely grated)
- ½tsp salt
- ½tsp bicarbonate of soda
- 1tsp paprika (optional)
- 2tsp freshly chopped rosemary (optional)
- 25g (1oz) butter (melted)
- 1 egg yolk
- 4tbsp warm water

Salt

Butter

Tools

- Large baking tray
- Large mixing bowl
- Wooden spoon
- Rolling pin
- 6cm (2½") cookie cutter
- Oven gloves

Baking tray

1 Preheat the oven to 200°C (400°F, gas mark 6). Lightly grease a large baking tray with some butter on a piece of baking paper to prevent the oatcakes from sticking to the tray.

2 Place the oatmeal, cheese, salt, bicarbonate of soda, paprika and rosemary in a large mixing bowl. Stir the ingredients together with a wooden spoon until they are mixed.

3 Stir in the butter, egg yolk and water to make a sticky dough. Place the dough on a lightly floured surface and use your hands to press the mixture together.

4 Roll out the dough very thinly to about 2mm (⅛") thick on a lightly floured surface. Using a 6cm (2½") cutter, cut out the biscuits. Gather up the trimmings and re-roll and cut out.

5 Place the biscuits on the baking tray. Place the tray on the top shelf of the oven and cook for 15 minutes. Remove the tray from the oven and allow the oatcakes to cool completely.

Chef's Tip

You can store the oatcakes in an airtight container for up to a week. Don't keep them any longer or they will start to go soft.

Orange and Seed Cookies

These oaty cookies are flavoured with tangy orange. The sunflower seeds are a great source of vitamins and minerals, as well as adding an extra crunch!

Makes
14

Prep
15 mins

Cooking
10 mins

Chef's Tip

To make smaller cookies, place heaped teaspoons instead of dessert spoons of the mixture on the trays and bake for 7–9 minutes.

Sunflower seeds

Porridge oats

Orange

Bowl

Ingredients

- 125g (4oz) porridge oats
- 75g (3oz) sunflower seeds
- 150g (5oz) self-raising flour
- 150g (5oz) butter (diced)

- Finely grated zest of 1 orange
- 2tbsp orange juice
- 150g (5oz) soft light brown sugar
- 2tbsp golden syrup

Butter

Golden syrup

Baking tray

Tools

- Three large baking trays
- Baking paper
- Large mixing bowl
- Wooden spoon
- Medium saucepan
- Dessert spoon
- Oven gloves
- Cooling rack
- Palette knife

Wooden spoon

1 Preheat the oven to 180°C (350°F, gas mark 4). Line three large baking trays with baking paper to prevent the cookies from sticking to them.

2 Place the oats, sunflower seeds and flour in a large mixing bowl. Stir the mixture with a wooden spoon until completely mixed together. Put the bowl to one side.

3 Place the butter, orange zest, juice, sugar and golden syrup in a medium saucepan. Heat the mixture over a low heat whilst stirring, until the butter and sugar have melted.

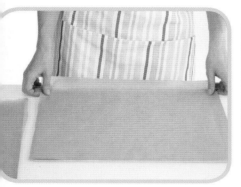

4 Carefully pour the butter mixture over the ingredients in the large mixing bowl and mix them together with the wooden spoon until thoroughly combined.

5 Place heaped dessert spoons of the mixture onto each tray. Leave a generous space between each biscuit, as they will spread. Bake for 8–10 minutes, until the cookies are golden.

6 Leave the cookies to cool on the tray for a few minutes, then transfer them to a cooling rack with a palette knife, to become crisp. They will keep in an airtight container for 2–3 days.

Star Biscuits

These biscuits make great gifts for your friends and family. You can use different shaped cutters for different themes, such as Christmas, Halloween or Valentine's Day.

Makes

15

Prep

25
mins

Cooking

12
mins

Chef's Tip

You can hang these biscuits as pretty decorations. Use a skewer to make the hole and thread them with ribbon.

Butter

Beaten egg

Ingredients

- 200g (7oz) plain flour
- 125g (4oz) butter (diced)
- 100g (3½oz) caster sugar
- 1tsp ground cinnamon
- Finely grated zest of 1 orange

- 1 medium egg, lightly beaten
- 2tbsp golden syrup

To decorate: ribbon, writing icing, edible silver balls or hundreds and thousands

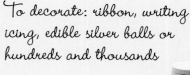
Flour

Orange

Golden syrup

Food processor

Tools

- Two large baking sheets
- Baking paper
- Food processor
- Small bowl
- Fork
- Rolling pin
- Star shape cutter
- Bamboo skewer
- Oven gloves
- Cooling rack

Skewers

1 Preheat the oven to 180°C (350°F, gas mark 4). Line two large baking sheets with baking paper. Pulse the flour and butter in a food processor, until the mixture resembles fine breadcrumbs.

2 Add the sugar, cinnamon and orange zest and pulse again. In a small bowl, beat together the egg and golden syrup with a fork then add this to the breadcrumb mixture.

3 Process the mixture in the food processor until it comes together in a ball. Lift the ball of dough out, wrap it in cling film and chill for 10 minutes in the fridge.

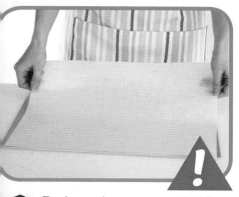

4 Roll out the chilled dough on a lightly floured surface, to 4–5mm (¼") thickness. Cut into stars using a shaped cutter. Re-roll and cut out more stars until you use up all the dough.

5 Place the stars slightly apart on the baking sheets and cook for 10–12 minutes. Allow to cool for 2 minutes and if they are decorations, poke a hole in the top of each using the skewer.

6 Transfer the stars to a cooling rack. When they are cool, decorate them as desired. Thread the holes with ribbon and tie the ends together if you are making them as decorations.

Flapjacks

Tasty crumbly oats mixed with sticky golden syrup and crunchy corn flakes make these flapjacks completely irresistible. Oats release energy slowly so you won't feel hungry again for a while.

Makes
16

Prep
10 mins

Cooking
25 mins

Chef's Tip

Don't be tempted to take the flapjacks out of the tin until they are completely cooled, or they will break up.

Sugar

Porridge oats

Ingredients

- 175g (6oz) butter (diced)
- 175g (6oz) soft light brown sugar
- 4tbsp golden syrup
- 350g (12oz) whole jumbo porridge oats
- 50g (2oz) corn flakes

Butter

Golden syrup

Oven gloves

Knife

Tools

- Large saucepan
- Wooden spoon
- 28cm x 18cm (11" x 7") tin
- Oven gloves
- Sharp knife

Saucepan

Chef's Tip

Cut the flapjacks into bars while they are still slightly warm otherwise they will be too hard to cut.

1 Preheat the oven to 180°C (350°F, gas mark 4). In a saucepan, gently melt the butter, sugar and golden syrup over a low heat, stirring with a wooden spoon until the sugar has dissolved.

2 Remove the saucepan from the heat and gently stir in the porridge oats and the corn flakes with the wooden spoon, until the mixture is thoroughly combined and sticky.

3 Tip the mixture into a 28cm x 18cm (11"x 7") tin and spread it into the corners. Gently press down with the back of the wooden spoon to make the top flat and even.

4 Bake the mixture for 25 minutes, or until golden and firm. Allow to cool for 10 minutes then cut it into bars. Leave to cool completely before lifting the bars out of the tin.

Variation

You can add 50g (2oz) dried fruit, such as chopped apricots, dried cranberries, blueberries or raisins for fruity flapjacks.

Makes
18

Prep
15
mins

Cooking
40
mins

Ginger and Pumpkin Slices

This sticky pumpkin and ginger cake is wonderfully dark and moist. It tastes even better the day after baking – if you can resist eating it for that long!

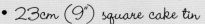
Square cake tin

Ingredients

Butter

Golden syrup

- 125g (4oz) butter
- 75g (3oz) dark muscovado sugar
- 150g (5oz) golden syrup
- 150g (5oz) black treacle
- 250g (9oz) pumpkin (grated)
- 300g (11oz) plain flour
- 1tsp bicarbonate of soda
- 2tsp ground ginger
- Two medium eggs (beaten)

Plain flour

Sugar

Tools

- 23cm (9") square cake tin
- Baking paper
- Medium saucepan
- Wooden spoon
- Large mixing bowl
- Oven gloves
- Chopping board
- Sharp knife

Oven gloves

Variation

If pumpkins are not in season, use grated butternut squash instead. They have a similar flavour as they are both part of the squash family of vegetables.

1 Grease the base of a 23cm (9") square cake tin with a bit of butter on some baking paper and line it with baking paper. Preheat the oven to 180°C (350°F, gas mark 4).

2 Place the butter, sugar, golden syrup and treacle in a medium pan and heat gently until the sugar has dissolved and the butter has melted. Remove it from the heat and allow to cool.

Chef's Tip

This cake improves
with keeping. Wrap it
in greaseproof paper and
keep it in an airtight
container for up to
a week.

3 In a large mixing bowl, add the grated pumpkin or butternut squash, plain flour, bicarbonate of soda and ginger. Mix thoroughly with a wooden spoon.

4 Stir in the treacle mixture and beaten eggs until combined, then pour into the greased and lined tin. Bake in the middle of the oven for 35–40 minutes, or until firm.

5 Allow the cake to cool in the tin. Once cool, carefully tip out onto a chopping board. Peel off the paper from the back and cut the cake into rectangles with a sharp knife.

35

Coconut Biscuits

Give oat biscuits a tasty tropical twist with creamy coconut. The bicarbonate of soda gives the biscuits a great crunchy texture.

Flour

Ingredients

- 75g (3oz) desiccated coconut
- 100g (3½oz) plain flour
- 100g (3½oz) caster sugar
- 100g (3½oz) porridge oats
- 100g (3½oz) butter (diced)
- 1tbsp golden syrup
- 1tsp bicarbonate of soda
- 2tbsp hot water

Large mixing bowl

Porridge oats

Butter

Tools

- Two baking trays
- Baking paper
- Large mixing bowl
- Wooden spoon
- Medium saucepan
- Dessert spoon
- Oven gloves
- Palette knife
- Cooling rack

Wooden spoon

Saucepan

Chef's Tip

These biscuits will store for up to a week in an airtight container.

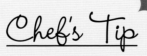

1 Preheat the oven to 180°C (350°F, gas mark 4). Line two baking trays with baking paper. Place the coconut, flour, sugar and oats in a mixing bowl and mix together with a wooden spoon.

2 Place the butter and golden syrup in a medium saucepan and heat over a low heat until melted. Stir the mixture with a wooden spoon to mix thoroughly.

Chef's Tip

A good way to measure out golden syrup is to lightly grease the tablespoon with a little oil. You'll find the golden syrup will just run off the spoon into the pan.

3 Mix the bicarbonate of soda with the hot water. Add it to the butter mixture in the saucepan. The bicarbonate will make the butter and golden syrup mixture fizz. Stir well.

4 Pour the butter mixture into the large mixing bowl and mix well. Spoon the mixture onto the baking trays with a dessert spoon, leaving room between each one for the biscuits to spread.

5 Bake the biscuits for 8–10 minutes on the top shelf of the oven until golden. Allow the biscuits to cool on the tray for five minutes, then transfer to a cooling rack to cool completely.

Chocolate Fudge Brownies

These delicious brownies are perfect – crisp on the outside and fudgy on the inside. Be careful not to overcook them as they should be gooey in the centre.

Chef's Tip

These brownies are very rich so you only need to serve them in small squares.

Variation

For nutty brownies, add 150g (5oz) chopped hazelnuts, walnuts, brazil or pecans. In Step 4, for double chocolate brownies, stir in 150g (5oz) white or milk chocolate chips or buttons.

Ingredients

Sugar

Butter

- 250g (9oz) butter
- 275g (10oz) 70% cocoa dark chocolate (broken into pieces)
- 275g (10oz) caster sugar
- Three large eggs
- 1tsp vanilla extract
- 225g (8oz) plain flour
- ½tsp salt

Chocolate

Eggs

Tools

- 23cm (9") square cake tin
- Baking paper
- Medium saucepan
- Wooden spoon
- Large mixing bowl
- Electric or hand whisk
- Metal spoon
- Oven gloves
- Cooling rack
- Sharp knife

Large mixing bowl

Square cake tin

1 Preheat the oven to 180°C (350°F, gas mark 4). Grease and line the base of a 23cm (9") square cake tin with baking paper to prevent the brownies from sticking.

2 Melt the butter and chocolate in a medium saucepan over a low heat, stirring occasionally with a wooden spoon. Remove the saucepan from the heat and allow to cool slightly.

3 In a large mixing bowl beat together the sugar, eggs and vanilla extract using an electric or hand whisk. Keep whisking until the mixture is pale and fluffy.

4 Whisk the chocolate mixture into the egg mixture until thoroughly combined, using the electric or hand whisk. Then stir in the flour and salt with a metal spoon.

5 Pour the mixture into the prepared tin and cook for 20–25 minutes in the middle of the oven, until the brownies are just set. The centre should be slightly gooey.

6 Leave the cake to cool for 10 minutes in the tin. Tip it onto a cooling rack. When it is completely cold, remove the baking paper and cut the brownies into squares.

Gingerbread

Gingerbread tastes great and smells wonderful as it bakes. This recipe can be used for regular shaped biscuits, pretty tree decorations or gingerbread people.

Makes
15

Prep
15 mins

Cooking
10 mins

Large mixing bowl

Golden syrup

Ingredients

- 350g (12oz) plain flour
- 2tsp ground ginger
- 1tsp bicarbonate of soda
- 125g (4oz) butter (diced)
- 150g (5oz) soft dark brown sugar
- 4tbsp golden syrup
- 1 medium egg (beaten)
- Sweets, currants and icing for decoration

Tools

- Two large baking trays
- Baking paper
- Large mixing bowl
- Wooden spoon
- Rolling pin
- Cutters of your choice
- Oven gloves

Wooden spoon

Butter

Sugar

Chef's Tip

These biscuits can stored in an airtight container for two days. To use them as decorations, use a skewer to punch a hole through the biscuit once it's cooked and thread a ribbon through the hole.

1 Preheat the oven to 180°C (350°F, gas mark 4). Line two large baking trays with baking paper. If you only have one tray, you will need to cook the biscuits in two batches.

2 Place the flour, ginger and bicarbonate of soda in a large bowl. Stir the ingredients together with a wooden spoon until they are thoroughly mixed.

3 Rub the butter into the mixture using your fingertips. Continue rubbing in the butter until the mixture resembles fine breadcrumbs. Stir in the sugar.

4 Stir in the golden syrup and egg, until the mixture starts to come together in a dough. Tip the dough mixture onto a lightly floured surface and knead it until smooth.

5 Roll out the dough on a lightly floured surface to a thickness of 5mm (¼"), then using your cutters, cut out the shapes. Re-roll the leftover dough and cut out more biscuits.

6 Place the biscuits on the baking trays and cook for 9–10 minutes or until golden. Allow the biscuits to cool on the trays. Decorate with sweets, currants and icing.

Doughs

Home-baked bread tastes fantastic and fills your kitchen with wonderful smells as it bakes! There are lots of special techniques you will need to know to bake your own bread. In this section you will learn all about the art and science of making dough.

Mixing

Dough is very sticky. Use a spoon or knife to mix it together at first, but then don't be afraid to get stuck in and knead with your hands. It's great fun!

Shaping bread

When you are making rolls or baguettes, you will need to shape the dough with your hands. Make sure your hands are clean and dusted with flour to prevent sticking.

Top Tip

Yeast is a type of fungus – but don't let that put you off! It is added to dough to make it rise and become stretchy. It needs heat to activate it.

Rising

Cover the dough with a damp tea towel or oiled cling film when it is rising to prevent a crust forming. Leave it in a warm place, such as near a warm oven or in an airing cupboard, as the yeast needs warmth to activate. Beware – if the heat is too high, it will kill the yeast.

How to knead

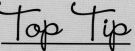

Secure the dough with one hand at the back, then place the heel of your other hand in the middle of the dough.

Push your front hand away from you, stretching the dough with it.

With your front hand, pick up the edge of the dough and fold it back on itself. Press it into a ball. Repeat.

Basic Bread

Makes
1 loaf

Prep
1¾ hours

Cooking
30 mins

Making bread is lots of fun, and the smell of baking bread will make your mouth water! This easy basic dough recipe can be made into delicious rolls or a traditional loaf. For tips on how to knead, turn to page 43. Replace the strong white bread flour with strong wholemeal bread flour if you want to make wholemeal bread.

Oven gloves

Ingredients

- 1½tsp active dried yeast
- 1tsp caster sugar
- 350ml (12floz) lukewarm water
- 500g (1lb 2oz) strong white bread flour
- 2tsp salt

Tools

- 900g (2lb) loaf tin
- Small mixing bowl
- Wooden spoon
- Sieve
- Clean damp tea towel
- Large mixing bowl
- Oven gloves
- Cooling rack

Bread flour

Salt

Loaf tin

Large mixing bowl

1 Lightly grease a 900g (2lb) loaf tin with butter. Place the yeast, sugar and a little of the water in a small bowl, stir well and leave in a warm place for 10 minutes, until frothy.

2 Sift the flour and salt into a large mixing bowl. Make a well in the centre and pour in the frothy yeast mixture and remaining water. Stir with a wooden spoon to form a dough.

3 Knead the dough on a lightly floured surface for 10 minutes. Place back in the bowl, cover with a damp tea towel and leave in a warm place for an hour or until doubled in size.

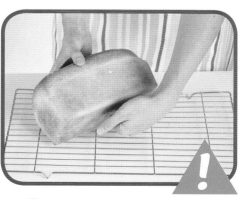

4 Preheat the oven to 220°C (425°F, gas mark 7). 'Knock back' the dough, by lightly punching it. (This knocks out the large air bubbles.) Then knead it lightly on a floured surface.

5 Shape the dough into a rectangle and tuck the ends under to fit into the tin. Place in the tin. Cover with the damp tea towel and leave to rise in a warm place for a further 30 minutes.

6 Place the tin in the centre of the oven. Bake for 30 minutes, or until risen and golden. Turn out the loaf and tap the base – it should sound hollow. Place on a cooling rack.

Variation

To make rolls: At Step 5 divide the dough into 8 balls. Flatten slightly. Place on a greased baking sheet, cover with a damp tea towel and leave to rise for 30 minutes. Brush the tops with milk, then sprinkle over some seeds (such as sesame or sunflower). Bake for 20–25 minutes.

Scones

Makes

8–10

Prep

10 mins

Cooking

12 mins

These traditional scones, served with jam and cream, will really hit the spot! The secret to making successful scones is not to handle the mixture too much or to add too much flour when rolling out the dough.

Pastry cutter

Pastry brush

Butter

Ingredients

- 225g (8oz) self-raising flour
- 1tsp baking powder
- Pinch of salt
- 50g (2oz) butter (diced)
- 50g (2oz) caster sugar
- 150ml (¼pt) milk
- Beaten egg or milk for brushing

To serve
- Whipped cream or butter, strawberry or raspberry jam

Large baking tray

Tools

- Large baking tray
- Sieve
- Large mixing bowl
- Wooden spoon
- Round-bladed knife
- Rolling pin
- 6cm (2½") pastry cutter
- Pastry brush
- Oven gloves
- Cooling rack

Milk

Jam

1 Preheat the oven to 220°C (425°F, gas mark 7). Lightly grease a large baking tray with some butter. Sift the flour, baking powder and salt into a large mixing bowl.

2 Using your fingertips, rub the butter into the flour mixture until the mixture resembles fine breadcrumbs. Stir in the sugar with a wooden spoon and mix together thoroughly.

3 Stir in the milk with a round-bladed knife until the mixture forms a soft dough and comes together in a ball. Gently knead the dough on a floured surface to remove any cracks.

Variation

For fruit scones, stir in 50g (2oz) currants, sultanas or raisins (or a mixture of these) with the sugar in Step 2 before you add the milk.

4 Roll out the dough to 2cm (¾") thickness, then using a 6cm (2½") pastry cutter, cut into circles. Gather up any trimmings, re-roll them and cut out more scones.

5 Place the scones on a baking tray, spacing them a little apart. Using a pastry brush, brush the tops with the egg or milk and cook for 10–12 minutes, or until risen and golden brown.

6 Transfer the scones to a cooling rack. (You can serve them warm or cold.) Cut them in half and spread with butter and jam or with whipped cream and jam.

Cheese and Onion Round

This savoury scone round makes a great accompaniment to soup or salad. It also tastes great on its own spread with a little butter or low-fat spread.

Chef's Tip

To make sure that the scone round rises well whilst baking, don't handle the dough too roughly or for too long in Step 4.

Beaten egg

Cheese

Ingredients

- 50g (2oz) butter (diced)
- 1 bunch spring onions, sliced (optional)
- 125g (4oz) self-raising flour
- 125g (4oz) wholemeal self-raising flour
- 1tbsp baking powder
- ½tsp salt
- 1tsp mustard powder
- 125g (4oz) mature Cheddar cheese (grated)
- 1 large egg
- 100ml (3½floz) milk
- Beaten egg or milk (for brushing)

Spring onions

Butter

Saucepan

Tools

Knife

- Baking tray
- Saucepan
- Wooden spoon
- Large mixing bowl
- Sieve
- Round-bladed knife
- Sharp knife
- Pastry brush
- Oven gloves
- Chopping board

1 Preheat the oven to 200°C (400°F, gas mark 6). Lightly grease a baking tray. Melt 25g (1oz) of the butter in a saucepan, add the spring onions and cook over a medium heat for 2–3 minutes.

2 Sift the flours, baking powder and salt into a bowl. Use your fingertips to rub the remaining butter into the flour, until the mixture resembles fine breadcrumbs.

3 Stir in the mustard powder, ⅔ of the cheese and the cooked spring onions and mix well. Beat together the egg and milk, then stir them into the flour mixture with a round-bladed knife.

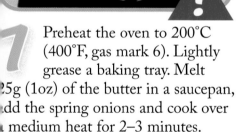

4 Gently knead the dough on a lightly floured surface to remove any cracks. Place on the baking tray and, using your hands, shape into a 18cm (7") round about 2cm (¾") thick.

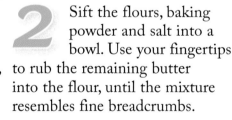

5 Using a sharp knife, divide the round into eight wedges, cutting deeply into the dough. Using a pastry brush, brush the tops with the egg or milk and sprinkle over the remaining cheese.

6 Cook the round for 20–25 minutes, or until risen and golden. (Cover the top with foil if it becomes too brown.) Place it on a chopping board and cut into wedges. Serve warm or cold.

Pizza Dough

It is really easy to make your own pizza dough and incredibly tasty! Just follow the recipe, then add pizza sauce and your favourite toppings to custom make a delicious homemade pizza.

Makes

1

Prep

1¼ hours

Cooking

15 mins

Salt

Large mixing bowl

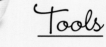

Rolling pin

Tools

- Large mixing bowl
- Wooden spoon
- Damp tea towel
- Baking sheet
- Rolling pin
- Oven gloves

Ingredients

- 225g (8oz) strong plain white flour
- ½tsp salt
- ½tsp fast-action dried yeast
- 150ml (¼pt) warm water
- 1tbsp extra-virgin olive oil
- Pizza toppings of your choice

Baking sheet

Flour

Olive oil

1 Place the flour, salt and yeast in a large mixing bowl and make a well in the centre. Using a wooden spoon, stir in the warm water and olive oil to form a dough.

2 Place the dough on a lightly floured surface and knead for 7–10 minutes until it is smooth and elastic. (For tips on how to knead turn to page 43.)

3 Place the dough in a lightly oiled bowl, cover with a clean damp tea towel and leave to rise in a warm place for an hour, or until the dough has doubled in size.

Variation

To give your pizza a herby zing, try adding a tablespoon of dried oregano in Step 1.

4 Preheat the oven to 220°C (450°F, gas mark 7). Lightly oil a baking sheet with some olive oil. 'Knock back' the risen dough to get rid of the air bubbles.

5 Knead the dough on a lightly floured surface for 2–3 minutes. Then, using a lightly floured rolling pin, roll out the dough to a 30cm (12") circle.

6 Place the pizza base on the baking sheet, then add the toppings of your choice. Bake for 10–15 minutes at the top of the oven until the dough is crisp and the toppings have cooked.

Multi-Grain Plait

Makes
1 loaf

Prep
15 mins

Cooking
30 mins

This multi-grain plait is fun to make and nutritious. If you want to make a white plait, just substitute the multi-grain bread flour for strong white bread flour.

1 Place the yeast, sugar and a little of the water in a small bowl. Stir well with a teaspoon and leave in a warm place for 10 minutes, until the mixture turns frothy.

2 Place the flour and salt in a large mixing bowl. Then rub in the butter with your fingertips until it is thoroughly mixed into the multi-grain flour.

3 Make a well in the centre and pour in the frothy yeast mixture and remaining water. Stir with a wooden spoon to form a dough, then use your hands to form a ball.

Ingredients

- 1½ tsp active dried yeast
- 1 tsp caster sugar
- 350ml (12floz) lukewarm water
- 500g (1lb 2oz) strong multi-grain bread flour
- 2 tsp salt
- 25g (1oz) butter (diced)
- Extra flour for dusting

Sugar

Flour

Large mixing bowl

Butter

Salt

Tools

- Small mixing bowl
- Teaspoon
- Large mixing bowl
- Wooden spoon
- Clean damp tea towel
- Baking sheet
- Knife
- Oven gloves

Wooden spoon

Baking sheet

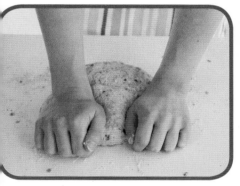

4 Knead the dough on a lightly floured surface for 10 minutes until the dough is smooth and elastic. (See page 43 for tips on how to knead dough.)

5 Place the dough in a lightly oiled bowl, cover with a clean damp tea towel and leave to rise in a warm place for an hour or until it has doubled in size.

6 Preheat the oven to 220°C (425°F, gas mark 7). Lightly grease a baking sheet. Place the dough on a lightly floured surface. 'Knock back' the dough to get rid of the air bubbles.

7 Shape the dough into a rectangle, then cut it into three equal pieces. Use your hands to roll each piece of dough into a 30cm (12") long sausage.

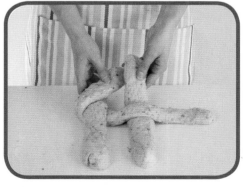

8 Make a 'H' with the dough pieces, weaving the middle piece over the piece on the left and under the piece on the right. Plait from the centre downwards. Turn the dough around and repeat.

9 Tuck the ends under and place on the baking sheet. Leave to rise for a further 30 minutes. Bake for 30 minutes, or until hollow when tapped. Remove from the tin and leave to cool.

Sticky Fruit Buns

Makes
10

Prep
2½ hours

Cooking
30 mins

These sweet, fruity buns are made with honey for extra stickiness! Traditional fruit buns are made with mixed spice, but you can leave this out if you prefer.

1 Place the flour, yeast and caster sugar in a large mixing bowl. Make a well in the centre of the mixture and crack the egg into the well. (To crack the egg, just tap it on the rim of the bowl.)

2 Melt the butter in a saucepan over a low heat then add the milk and warm through. Add this to the large bowl and bring together with a round-bladed knife.

3 Turn the dough onto a lightly floured surface and knead for 10 minutes. Return to the bowl, cover with a clean damp tea towel and leave in a warm place for about 1½ hours.

Clear honey

Raisins

Ingredients

- 350g (12oz) strong white bread flour
- 7g sachet fast-action dried yeast
- 25g (1oz) caster sugar
- 1 large egg
- 100g (3½oz) butter (diced)
- 175ml (6floz) milk

Egg   Brown sugar

For the topping

- 25g (1oz) butter (melted)
- 150g (5oz) mixture of raisins, currants and sultanas
- 25g (1oz) chopped mixed peel
- 50g (2oz) light soft brown sugar
- 1tsp ground mixed spice (optional)
- Grated zest of 1 lemon
- 1tbsp clear honey

Tools

- Two large mixing bowls
- Saucepan
- Round-bladed knife
- Clean damp tea towel
- 23cm (9") round shallow cake tin
- Baking paper
- Rolling pin
- Pastry brush
- Spoon
- Sharp knife
- Oven gloves
- Aluminium foil
- Cooling rack

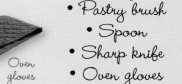
Knife

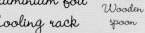

Oven gloves   Wooden spoon

4 Grease the base and sides of a 23cm (9") round, shallow cake tin and line the base with baking paper so the buns don't stick in the tin. Preheat the oven to 200°C (400°F, gas mark 6).

5 'Knock back' the dough, then tip it out onto a floured surface. Roll the dough out to a 30cm (14") square. Brush the melted butter all over it, using a pastry brush.

6 Mix together the dried fruit, mixed peel, brown sugar, mixed spice and lemon zest. Sprinkle on top of the pastry, leaving a 1cm (½") border. Gently roll up the dough into a sausage shape.

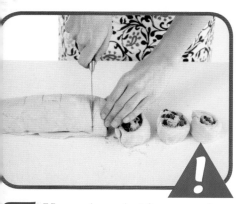

7 Use a sharp knife to cut the dough into ten pieces. Place them with their cut sides face up in the tin. Cover them with the clean damp tea towel and leave in a warm place for 35–40 minutes.

8 Bake the buns at the top of the oven for about 25–30 minutes until golden. If they start to become too brown, cover them with aluminium foil until cooked.

9 Carefully brush the buns with the honey, taking care not to burn yourself on the hot tin. Leave the buns to cool in the tin for 3–4 minutes. Then tip them out onto a cooling rack.

Italian Bread

This dimpled bread is known as focaccia and can be flavoured with herbs, cheese, sundried tomato or olives. It's so yummy, you'll keep coming back for more!

Serves
6–8

Prep
2 hours

Cooking
25 mins

Variation

For rosemary focaccia, mix 30ml (2tbsp) chopped fresh rosemary into the dough at Step 2. Add 100g (3½oz) of fresh Parmesan in Step 2 for cheese foccaccia.

1 Sift the flour into a large mixing bowl, add the salt and stir in the yeast with a large metal spoon. Lightly oil a baking tray to prevent the focaccia from sticking.

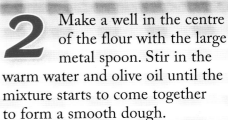

2 Make a well in the centre of the flour with the large metal spoon. Stir in the warm water and olive oil until the mixture starts to come together to form a smooth dough.

Bread flour

Ingredients

- 350g (12oz) strong white bread flour
- 7g sachet fast-action dried yeast
- ½tsp salt
- 175ml (6floz) warm water
- 50ml (2floz) olive oil

To finish
- 1tbsp olive oil
- Coarse sea salt for sprinkling

Salt

Olive oil

Baking tray

Sieve

Tools
- Sieve
- Large mixing bowl
- Large metal spoon
- Baking tray
- Clean damp tea towel
- Rolling pin
- Oven gloves

Rolling pin

Variation

For sundried tomato or olive focaccia, stir in 50g (2oz) olives or sundried tomatoes in oil, (drained and roughly chopped) at Step 2.

3 Transfer to a lightly floured surface and knead for 10 minutes until smooth and elastic. Place back in the bowl, cover with a clean damp tea towel and leave to rise in a warm place for an hour.

4 'Knock back' the dough to remove the large air bubbles, then place on a lightly floured surface. Using a rolling pin, roll out to a 20cm (8") circle about 1cm (⅖") thick.

5 Place the rolled-out dough on the oiled baking tray and cover with a clean damp tea towel. Leave the dough to rise in a warm place for 30 minutes.

6 Preheat the oven to 200°C (400°F, gas mark 6). Using your fingertips, make dimples all over the surface of the risen dough and drizzle with the olive oil.

7 Sprinkle the dough with the sea salt. Place in the oven on the middle shelf. Bake for 20–25 minutes until risen and golden. Delicious eaten warm!

Cornbread

This cornbread recipe is really simple to make and the sweetcorn and spring onions give it an unusual chunky, yet light texture.

Makes

24

Prep

10 mins

Cooking

30 mins

Variation

If you want to hot things up, try chilli cornbread! Simply add 1 finely chopped fresh red chilli in Step 2.

Chef's Tip

This cornbread makes a filling accompaniment to soup or salad. It also tastes great on its own!

Ingredients

- 125g (4oz) plain flour
- 125g (4oz) cornmeal or polenta
- 1tbsp baking powder
- 1tsp salt
- 5 spring onions, thinly chopped (optional)
- 150g (5oz) tinned sweetcorn
- 2 medium eggs
- 284ml carton buttermilk or natural yoghurt
- 100ml (3½floz) milk
- 50g (2oz) butter (melted and cooled)

Eggs

Polenta

Salt

Spring onions

Buttermilk

Measuring jug

Tools

- 20cm (8") square cake tin
- Baking paper
- Large mixing bowl
- Wooden spoon
- Measuring jug
- Small hand whisk
- Oven gloves
- Sharp knife

Large mixing bowl

1 Grease a 20cm (8") square cake tin and then line the base with baking paper to prevent the bread from sticking. Preheat the oven to 200°C (400°F, gas mark 6).

2 In a large mixing bowl, place the flour, cornmeal or polenta, baking powder, salt, chopped spring onions and sweetcorn. Mix together thoroughly with a wooden spoon.

3 In a measuring jug, whisk together the eggs, buttermilk (or yoghurt), milk and melted butter with a small hand whisk until they are thoroughly combined and frothy.

4 Pour the egg and milk mixture into the flour mixture in the large mixing bowl. Stir with a wooden spoon to combine all the ingredients thoroughly.

5 Pour the mixture into the prepared tin. Bake for 25–30 minutes until golden brown, and beginning to pull away from the sides of the tin. Allow to cool in the tin before cutting into squares.

Variation

For an extra indulgent treat, try topping the bread with a little grated cheese before baking.

Flatbreads

These flatbreads taste great served with hummous and dips, or with barbecued food. They are best eaten as soon as they are cooked, when they are still soft and warm.

Makes
6

Prep
1¼ hours

Cooking
3 mins

Variation

Try adding different ingredients to the flour mixture in Step 1 such as 1tbsp of freshly chopped rosemary, chopped spring onions or crushed garlic.

Large mixing bowl

Salt

Ingredients

- 250g (9oz) strong white bread flour
- 1tsp fast-action dried yeast
- ½tsp caster sugar
- ½tsp salt
- 175ml (6floz) lukewarm water

Sugar

Bread flour

Tools

- Large mixing bowl
- Wooden spoon
- Clean damp tea towel
- Rolling pin
- Non-stick frying pan
- Spatula or palette knife

Rolling pin

1 Place the flour, yeast, sugar and salt in a large mixing bowl and mix well with a wooden spoon. Make a well in the centre and stir in enough of the water to form a soft dough.

2 Place the dough on a lightly floured surface and knead for 5 minutes until smooth and elastic. (If you need tips on how to knead, turn to page 43.)

3 Return the dough to the bowl and cover with a clean damp tea towel. Leave it in a warm place for an hour or until the dough has doubled in size.

4 'Knock back' the dough (punch the dough with your fist) to remove the large air bubbles, then divide the dough into six equal chunks with your hands.

5 Knead each chunk lightly, on a lightly floured surface, to make a flatter round shape. Then roll out each piece of dough into a 13cm (5") circle with a rolling pin.

6 Preheat a frying pan. Add a flat piece of dough and cook for a minute, until golden underneath. Then flip it over and cook the other side for 30 seconds. Serve immediately.

Cakes

Cakes look fabulous but they are usually quite simple to make. Preparation is the key, so make sure you understand the basic techniques and your cakes will turn out just right.

Creaming

Mixing together sugar and butter is called creaming. If your butter is at room temperature you will find it much easier to mix.

Correct temperature

It is very important to use your ingredients at the correct temperature. Eggs should be at room temperature, otherwise they might curdle.

Testing a cake with a skewer

To test whether a cake is cooked properly, stick a skewer or knife in it. It will come out clean if the cake is cooked. If it has cake mixture on it, put the cake back in the oven for 5 minutes.

Top Tip

Do not be tempted to open the oven door while your cake is cooking – a sudden gush of cold air might make it sink in the middle! Wait until the cooking time is nearly finished before checking.

How to line a cake tin

1. Put the cake tin on top of some baking paper and draw round the bottom with a pencil or pen.

2. Cut out the shape with scissors and place the baking paper inside the tin.

Folding

Folding is a gentle method of mixing that keeps a cake light and airy. Use a metal spoon to fold the mixture over itself, instead of stirring it in a circle.

Simple Sponge Cake

Serves
6–8

Prep
10 mins

Cooking
30 mins

This cake is wonderfully light and moist. You can also make individual fairy cakes with this recipe (turn to page 122 for tips on decoration).

Ingredients

Butter

Milk

For the sponge
- 175g (6oz) butter (softened)
- 175g (6oz) caster sugar
- 3 medium eggs (beaten)
- 1tsp vanilla extract
- 175g (6oz) self-raising flour
- 1tsp baking powder
- 4tbsp raspberry or strawberry jam
- Icing sugar (for dusting)

For the buttercream
- 50g (2oz) butter (softened)
- 125g (4oz) icing sugar
- ½tsp vanilla extract
- 2tsp milk

Tools
Sieve

- 2 x 20cm (8") round cake tins
- Baking paper
- Large mixing bowl
- Sieve
- Electric or hand whisk
- Tablespoon
- Oven gloves
- Cooling rack
- Mixing bowl
- Wooden spoon
- Spatula

Wooden spoon

Jam

1 Preheat the oven to 180°C (350°F, gas mark 4). Grease two 20cm (8") round cake tins and line each base with baking paper so that the sponge cakes don't stick.

2 Place the butter, sugar, eggs and vanilla extract in a large bowl and sift over the flour and baking powder. Using an electric or hand whisk, beat all the ingredients together until thick.

3 Divide the mixture between the two tins, levelling the tops with the back of a tablespoon. Bake in the centre of the oven for 25–30 minutes, or until risen and firm to the touch.

4 Leave the cakes to cool in the tins for a few minutes, then turn them out onto cooling rack. Peel off the baking paper and allow the cakes to cool completely.

5 To make the buttercream filling place the butter, icing sugar, vanilla extract and milk in a mixing bowl. Beat them together with a wooden spoon until smooth and creamy.

6 Spread the flat side of one of the cakes with the jam. Spread the flat side of the other with the buttercream, then sandwich the two halves together. Dust with icing sugar.

Variation

This mixture will also make 20 fairy cakes, simply divide the mixture between paper cake cases and bake for 15 minutes.

Hard

Serves

12

Prep

35 mins

Cooking

30 mins

Double Chocolate Fudge Cake

If you are a chocolate lover, you will adore this cake! The dark chocolate sponge is filled and topped with a white chocolate icing.

Tools

Cake tins

- 2 x 20cm (8") cake tins
- Baking paper
- Two large mixing bowls
- Electric or hand whisk
- Sieve
- Spatula
- Oven gloves
- Cooling rack
- Heatproof bow
- Saucepan
- Wooden spoon
- Palette knife

Sieve

Ingredients

Eggs

For the cake
- 175g (6oz) butter (softened)
- 175g (6oz) soft brown sugar
- 150g (5oz) self-raising flour
- 25g (1oz) cocoa powder
- 1tsp baking powder
- ½tsp bicarbonate of soda
- 3 medium eggs (beaten)
- 100ml (3½floz) sour cream

For the icing
- 175g (6oz) white chocolate (broken into small pieces)
- 125g (4oz) butter
- 4tbsp milk
- 200g (7oz) icing sugar

Milk

To decorate: Grated chocolate, chocolate buttons and cocoa powder for dusting (optional)

Brown sugar

1 Preheat the oven to 170°C (325°F, gas mark 3). Grease and line the bases of the tins with baking paper. Place the butter and sugar in a mixing bowl and whisk together until combined.

2 Sift over the flour, cocoa powder, baking powder and bicarbonate of soda. Add the eggs and the sour cream and whisk with an electric or hand whisk until combined.

3 Divide the mixture between the two tins and level the tops. Bake for 25–30 minutes. Leave to cool slightly, then turn out onto a cooling rack. Remove the baking paper.

4 To make the icing, place the chocolate, butter and milk in a heatproof bowl over a saucepan of simmering water. Stir occasionally until the ingredients are melted and smooth.

5 Sift the icing sugar into a bowl, then pour over the melted chocolate mixture. Beat together with the whisk. Allow the icing to cool, then beat again until it forms soft peaks.

6 Use a little of the icing to sandwich the two cakes together. Spread the remaining icing over the top and sides of the cake. Decorate as desired and dust with cocoa powder.

Carrot Cupcakes

The grated carrots make these individual cakes perfectly moist and the yummy cream cheese frosting is a deliciously tangy topping.

Makes
18

Prep
10 mins

Cooking
20 mins

Butter

Carrots

Tools

- Bun tin
- 18 paper cases
- Large mixing bowl
- Electric or hand whisk
- Sieve
- Dessert spoon
- Oven gloves
- Cooling rack
- Wooden spoon
- Medium bowl

Bun tin

Electric whisk

Ingredients

- 175g (6oz) butter (softened)
- 175g (6oz) caster sugar
- 175g (6oz) self-raising flour
- 2tsp mixed spice
- 2 large eggs
- Grated zest of 1 orange and 1tbsp juice
- 2 medium carrots (peeled and coarsely grated)
- 50g (2oz) brazil or walnuts toasted and chopped (optional)

Frosting

- 200g (7oz) light cream cheese
- 2tbsp icing sugar
- 1tbsp orange juice
- 2tsp grated orange zest

Orange juice

Orange

1 Preheat the oven to 180°C, (350°F, gas mark 4). Place 18 paper cases in a bun tin. Most bun tins only have 12 holes so you may have to use two tins or cook your cakes in batches.

2 In a large mixing bowl, beat together the butter and sugar until they become pale and fluffy. Use an electric whisk if you have one. If not, then use a hand whisk.

3 Sift the flour and mixed spice into the bowl. Then add the eggs, orange juice and zest. Whisk together until all the ingredients are completely combined.

4 Stir the grated carrots and nuts (if you are using them) into the mixing bowl. Divide the mixture equally between the 18 paper cases using a dessert spoon.

5 Bake for 18–20 minutes in the middle of the oven until risen and golden brown. Remove from the oven using the oven gloves, and place on a cooling rack to cool completely.

6 Beat together all the frosting ingredients with a wooden spoon. Spread the frosting over the cooled cakes and decorate the cupcakes with extra orange zest.

Serves
10

Prep
15 mins

Cooking
1 hour

Banana and Buttermilk Cake

This cake has a lovely crumbly texture combined with crunchy nuts and soft gooey banana. It is a great way to use up any ripe bananas.

Variation

Replace the pecan nuts with chopped walnuts or brazil nuts or just leave them out.

Bananas

Ingredients

Butter

- 3 ripe bananas (broken into pieces)
- 1tsp lemon juice
- 100g (3½oz) pecan nut halves (optional)
- 100g (3½oz) butter (softened)
- 175g (6oz) soft brown sugar
- 2 medium eggs (beaten)

- 1tsp vanilla extract
- 250g (9oz) plain flour
- 1tsp salt
- 1tsp bicarbonate of soda
- 1tsp ground mixed spice
- 100ml (3½floz) buttermilk

For the topping
- 1 small banana (sliced)

Electric whisk

Lemon juice

Tools

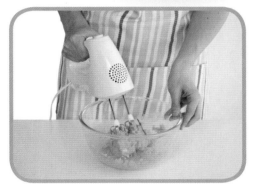
Loaf tin

- 900g (2lb) loaf tin
- Baking paper
- Two small bowls
- Fork
- Large mixing bowl
- Electric or hand whisk
- Sieve
- Metal spoon
- Oven gloves
- Aluminium foil
- Cooling rack

1 Preheat the oven to 180°C (350°F, gas mark 4). Grease and line the base of a 900g (2lb) loaf tin with baking paper. Mash the banana pieces with the lemon juice, using a fork.

2 Use your hands to break the pecan halves into small pieces into a bowl if you are adding nuts. If you don't like nuts, just leave this step out.

3 Place the butter and sugar in a large mixing bowl. Using an electric or hand whisk, beat them together until they are combined and become light and fluffy.

4 Beat in the eggs and vanilla extract, a little at a time. Stir in the banana mixture. Sift in the flour, salt, bicarbonate of soda and mixed spice and stir into the mixture with a metal spoon.

5 Stir in the buttermilk. Stir in the nuts if you are using them, saving a few. Pour the mixture into the tin and place the sliced banana on the top. Sprinkle over the saved nuts.

6 Bake in the oven for 50–60 minutes. If the cake becomes too brown, cover it with foil. Allow the cake to cool in the tin, then tip it out onto a cooling rack and remove the baking paper.

Marble Cake

Chocolate and orange cake mixtures are swirled together to make this spectacular marble-effect cake. This cake is lots of fun to make and you can change your swirling patterns every time you make it! Serve it cold or hot with custard or cream. Delicious!

Serves 25

Prep 10 mins

Cooking 30 mins

Orange

Butter

Ingredients

- 175g (6oz) butter (softened)
- 175g (6oz) caster sugar
- 175g (6oz) self-raising flour
- 3 large eggs
- Grated zest of 1 orange
- 2tbsp orange juice
- 2tbsp cocoa powder

Sugar

Tools

- 20cm (8") square cake tin
- Baking paper
- Large mixing bowl
- Electric or hand whisk
- Large spoon
- Sieve
- Round-bladed knife
- Oven gloves
- Chopping board
- Sharp knife

Electric whisk

Eggs

Square cake tin

1 Preheat the oven to 180°C (350°F, gas mark 4). Grease and line the base of a 20cm (8") square cake tin with baking paper to prevent the cake from sticking.

2 Place all the ingredients except the cocoa powder in a large mixing bowl. Using an electric or hand whisk, beat them all together until mixed and smooth.

3 Divide the mixture in half. Place large spoonfuls of one half of the mixture into the tin in each of the four corners and in the middle. Leave space between each spoonful.

Variation

Experiment by flavouring the cake with a teaspoon of vanilla or peppermint essence instead of orange.

4 Sift the cocoa powder over the remaining mixture in the bowl and whisk together until combined. Spoon the chocolate mixture into the spaces in the cake tin.

5 Gently drag a round-bladed knife through the mixtures to create a swirl effect with the brown and white mixtures. Don't overdo it, or you will mix the two colours together completely.

6 Bake the cake for 30 minutes, until well risen and springy. Allow it to cool in the tin, then remove it and peel off the baking paper. Cut it into 25 squares with a sharp knife.

Lemon Drizzle Cake

Serves
8

Prep
20
mins

Cooking
40
mins

It would be hard to find a more lemony cake than this one. The luscious lemon sponge has a contrasting crusty top made by pouring the lemon syrup over the cake while it is still warm.

Chef's Tip

Adding the lemon zest when you cream the butter and sugar helps to release the oils in the zest producing a much more lemony sponge.

Sugar

Small mixing bowl

Plain flour

Ingredients

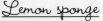
Lemons

Lemon sponge
- Finely grated zest of 2 unwaxed lemons
- 200g (7oz) butter (softened)
- 200g (7oz) caster sugar
- 3 medium eggs (beaten)
- 200g (7oz) self-raising flour (sifted)

Unsalted butter

Syrup
- Juice 4 lemons (about 100ml (3½floz))
- 75g (3oz) granulated sugar

Eggs

Large mixing bowl

Tools
- 20cm (8") round springform cake tin
- Baking paper
- Large mixing bowl
- Electric or hand whisk
- Metal spoon
- Oven gloves
- Small mixing bowl
- Cocktail stick
- Cooling rack

1 Preheat the oven to 180°C (350°F, gas mark 4). Butter a 20cm (8") round, springform cake tin and line the base with baking paper to prevent the cake from sticking to the tin.

2 Place the lemon zest, butter and caster sugar in a large mixing bowl and beat until the mixture is light and fluffy. You can use an electric or hand whisk.

3 Whisk in the eggs a little at a time. If the mixture starts to curdle, add 1tbsp of the flour. Use a metal spoon to fold in the flour then spoon the mixture into the prepared tin.

4 Bake the cake in the centre of the oven for 35–40 minutes. Put the lemon juice and granulated sugar in a small bowl. Leave in a warm place stirring occasionally.

5 When the cake is risen, golden and shrinking from the tin, remove it from the oven and prick all over with a cocktail stick about 20 times.

6 Drizzle the juice over the cake slowly. It will leave a crust as it sinks in. Allow the cake to cool in the tin for 10 minutes, then carefully transfer it to a cooling rack.

Savoury Muffins

Cheese and courgette give these savoury muffins a yummy flavour. They are perfect for a mid-morning snack or try one as part of your packed lunch!

Makes

12

Prep

10 mins

Cooking

25 mins

Variation

To make spinach and cheese muffins, replace the grated courgette with 180g (6oz) chopped baby spinach leaves in Step 3.

Milk

Plain flour

Sieve

Ingredients

- 2 medium-sized courgettes
- 125g (4oz) mature hard cheese (such as Cheddar)
- 275g (10oz) plain flour
- 1tbsp baking powder
- 1tbsp caster sugar
- 1tsp salt

- ½tsp ground black pepper
- 2 medium eggs (beaten)
- 175ml (6floz) milk
- 85g (3oz) lightly salted butter (melted)

Cheese

Muffin tin

Tools

- 2 x 6-hole or 12-hole muffin tin
- 12 muffin cases
- Grater
- Large mixing bowl
- Sieve
- Metal spoon
- Jug
- Fork or whisk
- Oven gloves
- Cooling rack

1 Preheat the oven to 375°F (190°C, gas mark 5). Line a muffin tin with 12 paper muffin cases. Trim the ends off the courgettes and grate them coarsely. Then grate the cheese.

2 In a large mixing bowl, sift together the flour and the baking powder. Stir in the sugar, salt and pepper with a metal spoon until they are thoroughly mixed together.

3 Add most of the grated cheese (but save a little to sprinkle over the top) and grated courgette. Using the metal spoon, mix well to combine all the ingredients.

4 In a jug, beat together the eggs, milk and butter with a fork or whisk. Pour them into the large mixing bowl and stir until just combined. The batter should be lumpy.

5 Using the metal spoon, divide the mixture equally between the 12 muffin cases and sprinkle each one with the remaining grated cheese.

6 Place the muffins in the centre of the oven and bake for 20–25 minutes until risen, golden and firm. Leave to cool on a cooling rack before serving them warm or cold.

Blueberry and Sour Cream Cake

Adding sour cream makes this pretty cake wonderfully moist and creamy. It can be decorated with fresh blueberries for an extra burst of fruity flavour!

Variation

Fresh raspberries will also work in this recipe. Replace the blueberries in Steps 4 and 6 with the same weight of raspberries.

Lemon

Ingredients

Sour cream

Cake tin

Metal spoon

For the cake
- 75g (3oz) butter (softened)
- 250g (9oz) caster sugar
- 284ml pot sour cream
- 2 medium eggs
- 2tsp vanilla extract
- 300g (11oz) self-raising flour
- 1tsp baking powder
- 225g (8oz) blueberries

For the frosting
- 200g (7oz) cream cheese
- Finely grated zest of 1 lemon
- 1tsp vanilla extract
- 1tbsp lemon juice
- 100g (3½oz) icing sugar
- 125g (4oz) blueberries

Tools
- 23cm (9") springform round cake tin
- Baking paper
- Two large mixing bowls
- Electric or hand whisk
- Sieve
- Metal spoon
- Cooling rack
- Small bowl
- Wooden spoon
- Oven gloves
- Palette knife

Butter

Blueberries

Large mixing bowl

1 Preheat the oven to 180°C (350°F, gas mark 4). Grease a 23cm (9") round springform cake tin and line the base with baking paper to prevent the cake from sticking.

2 Place the butter and caster sugar in a large mixing bowl. Using an electric or hand whisk, cream the butter and sugar together until they are light and fluffy.

3 Whisk in a little of the sour cream until the mixture is smooth. Then whisk in the remaining sour cream, eggs and vanilla extract until thoroughly combined and smooth.

4 Sift the flour and baking powder over the mixture and gently fold together using a metal spoon. Gently fold in the blueberries, then spoon the mixture into the tin. Level the top.

5 Bake for 45–50 minutes or until the cake feels firm. Leave the cake to cool in the tin for 10 minutes, then tip out onto a cooling rack and peel off the paper. Leave to cool completely.

6 Beat the cream cheese, lemon zest and juice with a wooden spoon in a bowl. Sift over the icing sugar and beat in. Spread the frosting on the cake and decorate with blueberries.

Cake Roll

Deliciously light sponge is combined with fruity jam in this classic cake. The technique can be tricky to master, so you might need to ask an adult to help you.

Serves 8

Prep 15 mins

Cooking 10 mins

Variation

For a chocolate cake roll, replace 25g (1oz) of the flour with cocoa powder. This variation is delicious filled with chocolate buttercream icing (see page 122).

1 Preheat the oven to 200°C (400°F, gas mark 6). Brush the base and sides of a 33cm x 23cm (13" x 9") tin with a little vegetable oil, then line with baking paper. Brush with a little more oil.

2 Whisk the eggs and sugar together in a bowl, using an electric whisk. Whisk for about 10 minutes until the mixture is light and frothy and the whisk leaves a trail when lifted.

Ingredients

Sugar

Eggs

Vegetable oil

- 1tbsp vegetable oil
- 3 large eggs
- 125g (4oz) caster sugar, plus extra
- 125g (4oz) self-raising flour

For the filling
- 5tbsp raspberry jam

Jam

Electric whisk

Tools

Knife

- 33 x 23cm (13 x 9") tin
- Pastry brush
- Baking paper
- Large mixing bowl
- Electric whisk
- Sieve
- Metal spoon
- Oven gloves
- Clean damp tea towel
- Sharp knife
- Palette knife

3 Sift the flour into the mixture, carefully folding at the same time with a metal spoon. Pour the mixture into the prepared tin and give it a gentle shake so that the mixture is level.

4 Place the filled tin on the top shelf of the oven. Bake for about 10 minutes or until the sponge is a golden brown and begins to shrink from the edges of the tin.

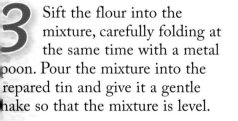

5 Lay out a damp tea towel on the work surface. Place a piece of baking paper a little bigger than the size of the tin onto the tea towel and sprinkle it with caster sugar.

6 Using oven gloves, tip the warm cake out onto the sugared paper so it is upside down. Take off the gloves and gently loosen the baking paper and peel it off.

7 Trim the edges of the sponge with a sharp knife. Make a score mark 2.5cm (1") from one shorter edge, being careful not to cut right through. This makes the cake easier to roll.

8 Leave the sponge to cool slightly, then spread the jam over it with a palette knife. Roll up the cake firmly from the cut end. Place the cake on a plate seam side down and serve in slices.

Orange and Poppy Seed Muffins

These scrumptious muffins have a zingy fresh orange taste and the poppy seeds add a slight crunch to the texture.

Makes

10

Prep

10 mins

Cooking

25 mins

Variation

Add 1tsp ground cinnamon instead of poppy seeds in Step 3 for cinnamon and orange muffins.

Oranges

Ingredients

Beaten egg

Sunflower oil

- 2 large oranges
- 275g (10oz) self-raising flour
- ½tsp bicarbonate of soda
- ½tsp salt
- 100g (3½oz) caster sugar
- 2tbsp poppy seeds (optional)
- 1 large egg (beaten)
- 90ml (3floz) sunflower oil

Orange icing
- 75g (3oz) icing sugar
- 2 tsp grated orange zest*
- 2-3tsp orange juice
(*use the zest from the oranges used in the main recipe)

Sugar

Muffin cases

Tools

- 2 x 6-hole or 12-hole muffin tin
- Paper muffin cases
- Grater
- Sharp knife
- Juicer
- Measuring jug
- Large mixing bowl
- Sieve
- Metal spoon
- Fork
- Oven gloves
- Cooling rack
- Small mixing bowl

Sieve

1 Preheat the oven to 375°F (190°C, gas mark 5). Line a muffin tin (or tins) with 10 paper muffin cases. Finely grate the zest from the oranges with the grater.

2 Cut the oranges in half and squeeze the juice into a jug, removing any pips. You should have about 180ml (6floz) orange juice. Add water to make it up to this amount if necessary.

3 In a large mixing bowl, sift the flour, bicarbonate of soda and salt. Stir in the caster sugar, poppy seeds and 1tbsp of the orange zest. Using a metal spoon, mix together.

4 Add the beaten egg and oil to the orange juice and beat together with a fork. Pour the mixture into the bowl and stir until just combined. Don't worry – the batter will be lumpy!

5 Spoon into the cases and cook in the centre of the oven for 20–25 minutes until well risen and golden. Leave to cool for a few minutes, then transfer to a cooling rack.

6 Sift the icing sugar into a small bowl, then add the orange zest and juice. Stir until you have a smooth icing. Drizzle over the muffins when they have completely cooled.

Tropical Fruit Cake

This cake is really simple to make. It uses pineapple and mango to add a tropical flavour, but you can use any of your favourite dried fruit.

Serves

12

Prep

15 mins

Cooking

1 hour

Variation

This recipe can be made into a traditional fruit cake by replacing the tropical fruit with currants, sultanas, more raisins and glacé cherries.

Raisins

Butter

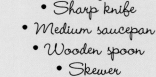
Loaf tin

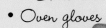

Tools

- 900g (2lb) loaf tin
- Baking paper or loaf tin liner
- Chopping board
- Sharp knife
- Medium saucepan
- Wooden spoon
- Skewer
- Oven gloves

Chopping board

Ingredients

- 250g (9oz) soft mixed dried tropical fruit e.g. pineapple, mango, papaya, apricots
- 100g (3½oz) raisins
- 1tsp mixed spice

- 125g (4oz) butter (diced)
- 125g (4oz) soft brown sugar
- 150ml (¼pt) cold water
- 225g (8oz) self-raising flour
- 1 egg (beaten)

Sugar

Apricots

Beaten egg

1 Grease and line the base of a 900g (2lb) loaf tin (or use a loaf tin liner). On a chopping board, carefully cut the tropical fruit into small pieces with a sharp knife.

2 Place the raisins, dried tropical fruit, mixed spice, butter, sugar and water in a medium saucepan. Warm over a low heat until the butter has melted, stirring with a wooden spoon.

3 Bring the butter and fruit mixture to the boil and allow it to simmer for 5 minutes. Then remove the saucepan from the heat and leave the mixture to cool completely.

4 Preheat the oven to 150°C (300°F, gas mark 2). When the mixture is cool, stir in the flour and the egg with the wooden spoon until combined. Then spoon it into the prepared tin.

5 Bake in the centre of the oven for 50–60 minutes, or until a skewer inserted into the middle comes out clean. Leave the cake to cool in the tin. When cool, serve in slices.

Chef's Tip

This cake tastes great served in thin slices, spread with a little butter.

Lime and Coconu Cupcakes

Give classic cupcakes a makeover with mouthwatering coconut and refreshing lime.

Makes 18

Prep 10 mins

Cooking 20 mins

Tools

- 12-hole bun tin
- 6-hole bun tin
- 18 paper cases
- Large mixing bowl
- Electric or hand whisk
- Metal spoon
- Oven gloves
- Cooling rack
- Small mixing bowl
- Sieve
- Teaspoon

Large mixing bowl

Bun tin

Ingredients

Sugar

- 125g (4oz) butter (softened)
- 125g (4oz) caster sugar
- Finely grated zest and juice of 2 limes
- 2 medium eggs
- 150g (5oz) self-raising flour
- 1tsp baking powder
- 50g (2oz) sweetened and tenderised or desiccated coconut

For the icing
- Finely grated zest and juice of 1 lime
- 175g (6oz) icing sugar
- Few drops green colouring (optional)
- 2tbsp sweetened and tenderised or desiccated coconut

Butter

Eggs

Flour

1 Preheat the oven to 180°C (350°F, gas mark 4). Line the bun tins with 18 paper cases. Use two 12-hole bun tins if you don't have a 6-hole tin or cook the cupcakes in batches.

2 In a large mixing bowl, whisk the butter, sugar and lime zest together using an electric or hand whisk until they are light and fluffy. Whisk in the eggs and lime juice.

3 Using a metal spoon, fold the flour, baking powder and coconut into the butter and sugar mixture. Divide the mixture between the paper cases. They should be about ⅔ full.

Variation

Instead of lime zest and juice, add 2tsp vanilla extract in Step 2. Stir a little vanilla extract and water in Step 5 instead of lime zest and juice.

4 Cook the cupcakes in the oven for 15–20 minutes until well risen and golden (cook them on the top shelf if you are cooking in batches). Transfer to a cooling rack and allow to cool.

5 Place ⅔ of the lime zest (saving some for decoration) and lime juice in a bowl and sift over the icing sugar. Stir until the icing is smooth, adding a little green colouring if you are using it.

6 Use a teaspoon to drizzle the icing over the tops of the cooled cupcakes and sprinkle over the coconut. Add the saved curls of lime zest to decorate.

Makes

10

Prep

10
mins

Cooking

25
mins

Oat and Honey Muffins

These fluffy light muffins are perfect for breakfast or a mid-morning snack because they are packed with nutritious oats and dried fruit.

Dried apricots

Muffin tin

Ingredients

- 250g (9oz) plain flour
- 1tbsp baking powder
- 100g (3½oz) porridge oats
- 125g (4oz) ready-to-eat dried apricots (chopped)
- 50g (2oz) soft light brown sugar
- ½tsp salt
- 2 medium eggs (beaten)
- 175ml (6floz) milk
- 75ml (3floz) sunflower oil
- 5tbsp clear honey

Tools

- 2 x 6-hole or 12-hole muffin tin
- 10 paper muffin cases
- Large mixing bowl
- Sieve
- Wooden spoon
- Large jug
- Fork
- Oven gloves
- Cooling rack

Muffin cases

Honey

Porridge oats

Variation

Don't like apricots? Just replace them with your favourite dried fruit, such as papaya or mango.

1 Preheat the oven to 375°F (190°C, gas mark 5). Line a muffin tin with 10 paper cases. Sift the flour and baking powder into a bowl and stir in the oats, apricots, sugar and salt.

2 Put the flour mixture to one side. In a large jug, beat together the eggs, milk, oil and honey with a fork until thoroughly mixed and frothy.

3 Pour the wet mixture in the jug over the dry ingredients in the bowl. Stir with a wooden spoon until the ingredients are just combined. The batter will be lumpy and quite runny.

4 Divide the mixture between the muffin cases, so they are ⅔ full and cook on the top shelf of the oven for 20–25 minutes. Leave in the tin for a few minutes, then transfer to a cooling rack.

Chef's Tip
These muffins taste great served with yoghurt or fresh fruit and an extra drizzle of honey.

Cocoa Mint Meringues

These delicious, cocoa-dusted meringues will melt in your mouth – they're crisp on the outside and soft in the middle! They are filled with lightly whipped peppermint cream and chocolate chips.

Chef's Tip

Try flavouring the whipped cream with vanilla or almond essence instead of peppermint. Or for plain meringues, just leave out the cocoa powder.

Ingredients

 Eggs

Double cream

- 2 large egg whites
- 100g (3½oz) caster sugar
- 2tsp cocoa powder (plus some extra for dusting)
- 150ml (¼pt) double cream
- 1tsp peppermint extract (optional)
- 1-2 drops green food colouring (optional)
- 50g (2oz) milk or plain chocolate chips

Sugar

Tools

Large mixing bowl

- Two large baking sheets
- Baking paper
- Large mixing bowl
- Electric or hand whisk
- Metal tablespoon
- Sieve
- Teaspoon
- Oven gloves

Electric whisk

1 Preheat the oven to 140°C (275°F, gas mark 1). Lightly grease two large baking sheets and line with baking paper. Whisk the egg whites in a bowl until they form stiff peaks.

2 Add the sugar to the egg whites a tablespoon at a time, whisking well with the electric or hand whisk after each spoonful. The mixture should be smooth, thick and glossy.

3 Sift the cocoa powder over the egg white and sugar mixture. Use a metal tablespoon to fold it over a few times until the mixture is streaked. (See page 63 for tips on folding.)

4 Using a teaspoon place heaps of the mixture onto the prepared baking sheets, spaced a little apart, until you have 0 meringues. Flatten each slightly with the back of the spoon.

5 Bake in the preheated oven for 1½ hours, or until the meringues peel away from the baking paper without much resistance. Leave them to cool on the baking sheets.

6 Whisk the cream, colouring and peppermint extract until thick. Stir in the chocolate chips. Spread the mixture on half of the meringues and sandwich with the other halves. Dust with cocoa.

Serves
8–10

Prep
20
mins

Cooking
35
mins

Upside-down Apple Cake

This fruity cake is fun to make and impressive to look at! Rings look prettier, but slices of apple or pineapple also work.

Chef's Tip
Use a sealed cake tin to prevent the cinnamon butter leaking out over the oven.

1 Preheat the oven to 180°C (350°F, gas mark 4). Grease the base and sides of a 20cm (8") round cake tin, 7.5cm (3") deep. The cake tin should not be a springform or loose-bottomed one.

2 Peel the apples with a peeler, then using a corer remove the cores from the centres. Cut each apple into 5 rings and place in the bottom of the tin, overlapping if necessary.

Butter

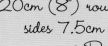
Sugar

Milk

Ingredients

For the topping
- 2 eating apples
- 50g (2oz) butter (diced)
- 50g (2oz) light muscovado sugar
- 1tsp ground cinnamon (optional)

Eggs

For the cake
- 125g (4oz) butter (softened)
- 125g (4oz) caster sugar
- 2 large eggs
- 125ml (4floz) milk
- ½tsp bicarbonate of soda
- 175g (6oz) self-raising flour

Tools
- 20cm (8") round cake tin with sides 7.5cm (3") deep
- Peeler
- Corer
- Sharp knife
- Chopping board
- Small mixing bowl
- Spoon
- Large mixing bowl
- Electric or hand whisk
- Sieve
- Spatula
- Oven gloves

Cake tin

Peeler

Variation

To make a pineapple upside-down cake, replace the apples with canned pineapple rings in natural juice. Drain the rings well on kitchen paper and miss out the cinnamon from the topping mixture.

3 In a small mixing bowl mix together the diced butter, sugar (and cinnamon if you are using it) and sprinkle the mixture over the apple rings in the bottom of the cake tin.

4 Place the butter and sugar in a large bowl. Using an electric or hand whisk beat them together until pale and fluffy. Whisk in the eggs, adding a little flour if the mixture starts to curdle.

5 Whisk in the milk and bicarbonate of soda a little at a time, with some of the flour. Sift over the remaining flour and stir the mixture together until they are just combined.

6 Pour the cake mixture over the apple rings and spread evenly, using a spatula. Bake the cake in the centre of the oven for 30–35 minutes, until golden and firm to the touch.

7 Cool the cake in the tin for 5 minutes, then turn it out. Serve the apple upside-down cake in slices. It can be eaten cold or warm with custard, cream or ice cream.

Mini Muffins

These bite-sized treats have the delicious combination of tasty banana and melt-in-your-mouth chocolate chips. They are perfect for lunch boxes or for a light snack.

Makes
48

Prep
10 mins

Cooking
12 mins

Ingredients

- 280g (10oz) plain flour
- 1tbsp baking powder
- ½tsp salt
- 125g (4oz) caster sugar
- 2 large ripe bananas (peeled and roughly chopped)
- 1 large egg
- 240ml (8floz) milk
- 85g (3oz) butter (melted)
- 175g (6oz) milk chocolate chips or chunks

Sugar

Egg

Butter

Bananas

Tools

- 24-hole mini-muffin tin
- Mini-muffin paper cases (optional)
- Large mixing bowl
- Sieve
- Wooden spoon
- Small mixing bowl
- Fork
- Small hand w
- Jug
- Teaspoon
- Oven gloves

Fork

Large mixing bowl

1 Preheat the oven to 200°C (400°F, gas mark 6). Grease a 24-hole mini-muffin tin with butter (or line it with mini-muffin paper cases) to stop the muffins from sticking.

2 In a large mixing bowl, sift together the flour, baking powder and salt. Stir in the sugar with a wooden spoon until all the ingredients are thoroughly mixed.

3 In a small mixing bowl, mash the two ripe bananas with a fork until nearly smooth but with a few lumps remaining – this will give a nice texture to the muffins.

Variation

Try using white chocolate chips or chunks in Step 5 instead of milk chocolate chips. You could also experiment with other flavours of chocolate.

4 In a jug, whisk together the egg, milk and butter, then pour onto the mashed banana in the bowl. Stir the ingredients together until they are combined thoroughly.

5 Add the egg and banana mixture to the flour mixture. Stir the ingredients together with a wooden spoon to just combine, then fold in the chocolate chips or chunks.

6 Spoon the mixture into the tin and bake for 10–12 minutes. Leave the cakes to cool in the tin then remove them and repeat with the remaining ingredients to make a second batch.

Baked Raspberry Cheesecake

Serves
8

This baked cheesecake is so simple to make. You could replace the raspberries with blueberries if you prefer. Serve at a party for your friends or family.

Prep
15 mins

Cooking
40 mins

Chilling
3¼ hours

Variation

Replace the digestive biscuits with chocolate chip cookies. Delicious!

Ingredients

- 200g (7oz) digestive biscuits
- 50g (2oz) butter
- 600g (1lb 4oz) cream cheese
- 142ml pot sour cream
- 25g (1oz) cornflour
- 75g (3oz) icing sugar (sifted)
- 3 medium eggs
- 1tsp vanilla extract
- 225g (8oz) fresh raspberries

To serve
- Fresh raspberries
- Icing sugar (for dusting)

Butter

Raspberries

Cake tin

Tools

- Food bag
- Rolling pin or food processor
- Chopping board
- Wooden spoon
- Saucepan
- 20cm (8") springform round cake tin
- Large mixing bowl
- Electric or hand whisk
- Metal spoon
- Baking tray
- Oven gloves

Rolling pin

Saucepan

Eggs

1 Preheat oven to 170°C (325°F, gas mark 3). Place the biscuits in a food bag and crush them with a rolling pin. (You could also do this with a food processor.).

2 Melt the butter in a saucepan and stir in the crushed biscuits. Press the biscuit mixture into the base of the tin with the back of a spoon. Chill in the fridge for 15 minutes.

3 Place the cream cheese and sour cream in a large mixing bowl. Using an electric or hand whisk, beat the mixture until smooth. Then beat in the cornflour and icing sugar.

4 Add the eggs and vanilla extract to the bowl and whisk until smooth. Using a metal spoon, carefully stir in the raspberries. Pour this mixture over the biscuit base.

5 Place the cake on a baking tray and bake for 35–40 minutes in the middle of the oven until just set. Leave it to cool, then chill the cake in the fridge for 2–3 hours or overnight.

6 Carefully remove the cake from the springform tin and decorate with the fresh raspberries. Dust the cheesecake with icing sugar, and serve it in slices.

Pastry

Pastry is made using flour, fat and water and there are many different types. Puff, shortcrust and filo pastry can be bought fresh or frozen in the shops, and work well in the following recipes. If you have time, you can make your own shortcrust pastry using the simple recipe opposite.

Different types of pastry

Choux pastry is used for profiterôles and éclairs. Shortcrust pastry is used for making pies and tarts and can be sweet or savoury. Puff pastry is used for pies and baked slices. Filo is lots of thin layers of pastry and is used for sweet and savoury pies and tarts.

Top Tip

When rolling out pastry, use a cool surface and dust the surface and rolling pin with a little flour. Glazing pastry with beaten egg or milk will give it an appetising sheen.

How to make shortcrust pastry

1. In a bowl, sift 225g (8oz) plain flour with a pinch of salt. Add 125g (4oz) diced butter and rub this into the flour using your fingertips.

2. Stir in 3–4tbsp of cold water with a round-bladed knife until the mixture begins to stick together and form a dough.

3. Knead the dough lightly on a floured work surface until smooth. Wrap it in cling film and chill it for 30 minutes before you use it.

Top Tip

Pastry will be much easier to handle if you make sure your hands are cold when making it. Hot hands will make the butter in the pastry melt.

Baking blind

Baking blind is when you bake a pastry case with baking beans inside it instead of the filling. This seals the pastry and stops it from rising. You then bake it again with the filling inside. If you don't have baking beans, you can use scrunched up aluminium foil.

Chocolate Profiterôles

Serves

6

Prep

25 mins

Cooking

25 mins

You won't be able to resist these light and fluffy profiterôles. Topped with warm chocolate sauce, they're simply delicious!

1 Preheat the oven to 200°C (400°F, gas mark 6). Grease a baking sheet and sprinkle it with a little cold water. (This will generate steam in the oven and help the choux pastry to rise.)

2 Place the butter and cold water in a medium saucepan and heat gently until the butter has melted. Then turn up the heat and bring them quickly to the boil.

3 Remove the saucepan from the heat and add all the flour at once. Then beat the melted butter and flour together with a wooden spoon until the mixture comes together.

Plain flour

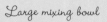
Eggs

Ingredients

Choux pastry
- 150ml (¼pt) cold water
- 50g (2oz) butter (diced)
- 75g (3oz) plain flour (sifted)
- 2 medium eggs (beaten)

Filling
- ½tsp vanilla extract
- 300ml (½pt) double cream

Chocolate sauce
- 125g (4oz) plain chocolate (broken into small pieces)
- 25g (1oz) butter
- 2tbsp golden syrup

Saucepan

Large mixing bowl

Chocolate

Tools
- Baking sheet
- Two medium saucepans
- Wooden spoon
- Dessert spoon
- Oven gloves
- Knife
- Electric or hand whisk
- Large mixing bowl
- Teaspoon
- Heatproof bowl

Wooden spoon

4 Allow the mixture to cool for a couple of minutes. Then beat in the eggs with an electric whisk or wooden spoon, a little at a time, until the mixture becomes smooth and shiny.

5 Use a dessert spoon to place 12 golf ball-sized balls of the pastry on to the baking sheet. Bake the profiterôles at the top of the oven for 20–25 minutes.

6 Using oven gloves, take the cooked profiterôles out of the oven. Make a slit in the side of each with a knife to let the steam out, taking care not to burn your fingers. Allow to cool.

7 Add the vanilla extract and the cream to a large bowl. Whip them to form soft peaks using the electric or hand whisk. Then use the teaspoon to spoon the cream into the buns.

8 Place the chocolate, butter and golden syrup into a heatproof bowl. Place the bowl over a saucepan of simmering water and gently melt the contents. Stir well.

9 Carefully spoon the chocolate sauce over the profiterôles with a dessert spoon. Then serve immediately with any remaining sauce.

Cherry and Berry Pie

Serves 6-8

Prep 45 mins

Cooking 30 mins

This pie is really easy to make – you simply scrunch up ready-prepared puff pastry and fill with your favourite berry fruits! You can serve it with a scoop of vanilla ice cream or cream.

Raspberries

Ingredients

Beaten egg

- 500g (1lb 2oz) ready-prepared puff pastry
- 1 egg (beaten)
- 2tbsp semolina
- 650g (1lb 6oz) mixed berries e.g. stoned cherries, blueberries, raspberries, red and blackcurrants
- 2tbsp caster sugar
- Icing sugar (for dusting)

Blueberries

Tools

- Rolling pin
- 30cm (12") plate
- Sharp knife
- Baking sheet
- Pastry brush
- Teaspoon
- Large mixing bowl
- Large metal spoon
- Oven gloves

Knife

Pastry brush

Sugar

1 Preheat the oven to 200°C (400°F, gas mark 6). Roll out the pastry on a lightly floured surface. Cut around a 30cm (12") plate with a sharp knife to make a circle.

2 Place the pastry circle on a baking sheet. Use a pastry brush to spread the beaten egg on the pastry, then sprinkle over 1tbsp of the semolina with a teaspoon.

3 In a large mixing bowl, place the mixed berries, remaining semolina and 1tbsp caster sugar. Use a large metal spoon to gently mix together, taking care not to crush the berries.

4 Pile the fruit in the centre of the pastry, away from the edge. Scrunch up the edges of the pastry, bringing them towards the centre, but leaving the middle exposed.

5 Brush the scrunched pastry edges with more beaten egg and sprinkle the pastry with the remaining sugar. Chill for 30 minutes in the fridge.

6 Bake the pie at the top of the oven for 30 minutes until golden. If the pastry starts to become too brown, cover the pie with foil. Dust with icing sugar and serve in slices.

Chef's Tip
You can use defrosted frozen berries or any drained tinned fruit if fresh berries are not in season.

Chocolate Tart

This is perfect for chocoholics! This chocolate tart has a tangy orange pastry base. It can be served warm or cold with a dollop of ice cream or cream.

Serves
8

Prep
20 mins

Cooking
45 mins

Variation

Any flavour of jam works well spread on the pastry base instead of orange marmalade in Step 3.

1 Preheat the oven to 190°C (375°F, gas mark 5). Using a rolling pin, roll out the pastry on a lightly floured surface and use it to line the flan tin. Chill for 15 minutes.

2 Prick the base with a fork, line with baking paper and fill with baking beans or scrunched up aluminium foil. Place on the baking tray and bake on the top shelf of the oven for 15 minutes.

Egg whites

Double cream

Saucepan

Ingredients

- 350g (12oz) ready-prepared shortcrust pastry
- 4tbsp orange marmalade
- 200g (7oz) milk chocolate (broken into pieces)
- 2 large eggs (beaten)
- 50g (2oz) caster sugar

- 150ml (¼pt) double cream
- Cocoa powder (for dusting)

Tools

- Rolling pin
- 23cm (9") loose bottomed flan tin
- Fork
- Baking paper
- Baking beans or aluminium foil
- Baking tray

- Metal spoon
- Heatproof bowl
- Small saucepan
- Large mixing bowl
- Electric or hand whisk
- Wooden spoon
- Oven gloves

Heatproof bowl

Milk chocolate

Chef's Tip

Placing the tin on a baking tray will help to make the pastry base crisp.

3 Remove the paper and beans from the case and return it to the oven for a further 5 minutes, until golden. Whilst the pastry is still warm, spread the base with the marmalade.

4 Reduce the oven temperature to 160°C (325°F, gas mark 3). Melt the chocolate in a heatproof bowl, over a saucepan of simmering water, whilst stirring. Allow to cool slightly.

5 In a large mixing bowl, place the eggs and sugar and whisk with an electric or hand whisk until pale and fluffy. Whisk in the chocolate until thoroughly combined.

6 Stir in the cream with a wooden spoon. Pour the mixture into the tart case. Bake for about 25–30 minutes on the top shelf of the oven until the tart has just started to set.

7 Remove the tart from the oven. It will continue to set as it cools. Dust with cocoa powder. Serve in slices with a scoop of vanilla ice cream, pouring cream or crème frâiche.

Lemon Meringue

This family favourite has crunchy pastry layered with a tangy lemon filling and a soft meringue topping. It's a taste sensation!

Serves

6

Prep

10 mins

Cooking

55 mins

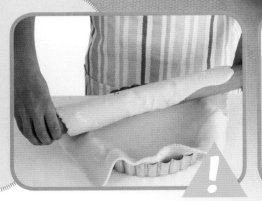

1 Preheat the oven to 190°C (375°F, gas mark 5). Roll out the pastry with a rolling pin on a lightly floured surface to about 25cm (10"). Line the flan tin with the pastry and chill for 15 minutes.

2 Prick the pastry case base with a fork, line with baking paper and fill with baking beans or scrunched aluminium foil. Place on a baking tray and bake for 15 minutes.

3 Remove the paper and beans from the pastry case and return to the oven for a further 5 minutes until golden. Then reduce the oven to 150°C (300°F, gas mark 2).

Lemons

Ingredients

Butter

Ingredients

- 175g (6oz) ready-prepared shortcrust pastry (or see p.99 for a recipe)

For the filling
- 3tbsp cornflour
- 150ml (¼pt) cold water
- 2 large lemons
- 75g (3oz) caster sugar

- 25g (1oz) butter
- 2 large egg yolks

For the topping
- 2 large egg whites
- 100g (3½oz) caster sugar

Eggs

Tools

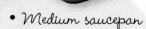
Baking tray

- Rolling pin
- 19cm (7½") loose-bottomed round fluted tin
- Fork
- Baking paper
- Baking beans or aluminium foil
- Baking tray
- Oven gloves

- Medium saucepan
- Grater
- Sharp knife
- Chopping board
- Jug
- Wooden spoon
- Large mixing bowl
- Electric or hand whisk
- Tablespoon

Heatproof bowl

4 Mix the cornflour and water together in the saucepan. Grate the zest from the lemons, then cut them in half and squeeze the juice into a jug, until you have 150ml (¼pt).

5 Add the lemon zest and juice to the saucepan, then slowly bring to the boil, stirring continuously with a wooden spoon. Simmer, still stirring, until the mixture thickens.

6 Remove the saucepan from the heat and stir in the sugar and butter. Let the mixture cool slightly, then beat in the egg yolks. Pour the mixture into the pastry case.

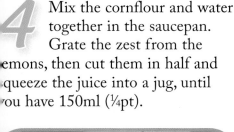

7 In a clean mixing bowl, whisk the egg whites with an electric or hand whisk until they form stiff peaks. Then whisk in the sugar 1tbsp at a time, until the mixture is thick and glossy.

8 Spoon the meringue mixture over the lemon mixture, leaving the rim of the pastry uncovered. Make peaks in the meringue with the back of the spoon, if you like.

9 Place the pie on the top shelf of the oven and bake for 30–35 minutes, or until the meringue is crisp and golden. Serve cold or warm with cream or ice cream.

Banoffee Pie

This divinely decadent caramel and banana pie is definitely for those with a sweet tooth!

Serves
8

Prep
20 mins

Cooking
20 mins

Chilling
1½ hours

Chef's Tip

For a really speedy banoffee pie, use a can of shop-bought toffee sauce.

Ingredients

Brown sugar

Bananas

For the base
- 250g (9oz) digestive biscuits
- 125g (4oz) butter

For the filling
- 125g (4oz) butter (diced)
- 125g (4oz) light soft brown sugar
- 397g (14oz) can sweetened condensed milk

- 150ml (¼pt) double cream
- 2 bananas (sliced)

To decorate: grated milk chocolate or flaky chocolate bar and slices of banana

Chocolate

Food processor

Tools

Flan tin

- Food processor or food bag and rolling pin
- Non-stick saucepan
- Wooden spoon
- 19cm (7½") loose-bottomed fluted flan tin, 4cm (1½") deep
- Large mixing bowl
- Electric or hand whisk
- Spoon

1 Place the biscuits in a food processor and process until smooth. If you don't have a food processor, place the biscuits in a food bag and crush them with a rolling pin.

2 Melt the butter for the base in a saucepan, then stir in the crushed biscuits with a wooden spoon. Press the mixture into the base and sides of the tin. Chill the base for 30 minutes.

3 Place the diced butter and sugar in the saucepan over a low heat, and stir until the butter has melted. Add the condensed milk and gently bring to the boil, stirring continuously.

4 Boil the butter, sugar and condensed milk for 5 minutes, stirring continuously until it is a pale caramel colour. Pour over the biscuit base and chill for 1 hour.

5 In a large mixing bowl, whip the cream with an electric or hand whisk until it forms soft peaks. Arrange the banana slices over the toffee, then spoon over the whipped cream.

6 Decorate the top of the pie with extra sliced banana and some grated milk chocolate. Serve the pie in slices. Keep chilled and eat within two days.

Medium

Makes

4

Chicken and Ham Pies

These yummy pies have tender chicken and ham, cooked in a creamy sauce and topped with golden puff pastry.

Prep

15 mins

Cooking

40 mins

Chef's Tip

If you don't have individual pie dishes, use a large ovenproof dish to make one large pie.

1 Place the butter, flour, stock and milk in a medium saucepan. Cook over a moderate heat, and continue whisking with the balloon whisk until the mixture starts to thicken.

2 Bring to the boil, then reduce the heat and add the crème fraîche and herbs. Season to taste with salt and freshly ground black pepper, then simmer for 2–3 minutes.

3 Heat the oil in a frying pan and add the chicken and onion. Cook for 3–4 minutes, stirring occasionally, until the onion has softened and the chicken has browned.

Ingredients

Stock

Peas

- 25g (1oz) butter
- 25g (1oz) plain flour
- 300ml (½pt) chicken stock
- 100ml (3½floz) milk
- 2tbsp crème fraîche
- 1tsp dried mixed herbs
- Salt and black pepper
- 1tbsp vegetable oil
- 1 small onion (sliced)

- 350g (12oz) chicken breast (cubed)
- 125g (4oz) cooked ham (cubed)
- 100g (3½oz) frozen peas
- 350g (12oz) ready-prepared puff pastry
- 1 egg (beaten)

Frying pan

Tools

- Medium saucepan with lid
- Balloon whisk
- Frying pan
- Wooden spoon
- Four individual pie dishes
- Rolling pin
- Sharp knife
- Pastry brush
- Oven gloves

Whisk

Butter

Beaten egg

4 Stir the chicken and onions into the sauce, then cover and simmer for 10 minutes. Remove the pan from the heat and stir in the ham and peas.

5 Preheat the oven to 200°C (400°F, gas mark 6). Allow the mixture to cool slightly, then divide it between four small individual pie dishes or one large one.

6 Roll out the pastry on a lightly floured surface, then cut out four circles, slightly larger than the top of the pie dishes. Use the scraps to make thin strips to cover the edges of the pie dishes.

7 Brush the edges of the pie dishes with the egg, then press on the strips of pastry. Brush with egg again, then place the pastry lids on top. Use your fingers to seal the edges of pastry together.

8 Brush the tops with egg and make a cross in the top of each pie to allow the steam to escape. Cook for 20 minutes at the top of the oven, until the pastry is puffed and golden.

Variation

Use vegetable stock in Step 1. In Steps 3 and 4, omit the chicken and ham. Simmer the sauce for 5 minutes and add 350g (12oz) cooked potatoes, carrots and parsnip, and 75g (3oz) sweetcorn when you add the peas.

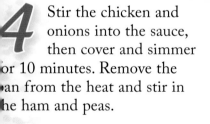

Serves
6

Prep
10 mins

Cooking
20 mins

Tomato and Basil Tart

This tart looks so impressive nobody will guess how simple it is to make! Serve it with salad and crusty bread for a delicious weekend lunch.

Rolling pin

Tools

- Rolling pin
- Baking sheet
- Sharp serrated knife
- Chopping board
- Large mixing bowl
- Wooden spoon
- Oven gloves

Chopping board

Beaten egg

Ingredients

- 375g (12oz) ready-prepared puff pastry
- 250g (9oz) cherry tomatoes
- 250g (9oz) ricotta cheese
- 2 large eggs (beaten)
- 2tbsp freshly chopped basil
- 25g (1oz) Parmesan cheese (grated)
- Salt and black pepper

Cherry tomatoes

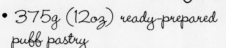

1 Preheat the oven to 200°C (400°F, gas mark 6). Roll out the pastry, using a rolling pin on a lightly floured surface to a rectangle measuring about 25cm x 38cm (10" x 15").

2 Place on a large flat baking sheet and using a sharp knife score a 2.5cm (1") border along the sides of the rectangle, being careful not to cut all the way through.

3 Place the cherry tomatoes on a chopping board and use a sharp knife to cut the tomatoes in half. A knife with a serrated edge will make it easier to cut them.

4 In a large mixing bowl, beat together the ricotta cheese, eggs, basil and Parmesan cheese with a wooden spoon, until combined. Season with a little salt and freshly ground black pepper.

5 Spoon this mixture inside the marked edge and scatter over the tomatoes. Cook in the centre of the oven for 20 minutes until the pastry is risen and golden and the filling cooked.

Chef's Tip

To make this recipe even speedier, you could buy ready-rolled puff pastry already in the shape of a rectangle!

Makes

4

Prep

15
mins

Cooking

25
mins

Filo and Spinach Tarts

The soft and creamy filling contrasts with the light crispy layers of filo pastry in this mouthwatering recipe for cheese and spinach tarts.

Variation

Replace the grated cheese with crumbled Feta cheese if you prefer.

Ingredients

Cheese

Beaten egg

- 1 tbsp sunflower oil
- 100g (3½oz) baby spinach leaves (washed)
- 125g (4oz) soft cream cheese
- 25g (1oz) Cheddar or Parmesan cheese (grated)

- 1 medium egg (beaten)
- Salt and freshly ground black pepper
- 16 x 12.5cm (5") squares filo pastry

Salt   Pepper

Tools

Knife

- Pastry brush
- 6-hole muffin tin
- Chopping board
- Sharp knife
- Large mixing bowl
- Wooden spoon
- Dessert spoon
- Oven gloves

Chopping board

1 Preheat the oven to 180°C (350°F, gas mark 4). Use a pastry brush to apply oil to four muffin tin holes. Place the spinach on a chopping board and chop roughly, using a sharp knife.

2 Place the cream cheese in a bowl and beat with a wooden spoon until smooth. Then beat in the grated cheese and egg until combined. Season well, then stir in the spinach.

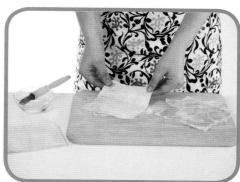

3 Brush one of the pastry squares with oil. Place another square over the top at an angle to make a star shape. Repeat with two more squares of pastry, brushing each with oil.

4 Gently press the layers of filo pastry into one of the holes of the muffin tin, and shape it to fit the hole. Repeat with the remaining pastry until you have four tarts.

5 Use a dessert spoon to fill each pastry case with the spinach mixture. Press it down with the spoon. Bake for 25 minutes until the pastry has browned and the filling has set.

6 Remove the tarts from the oven and allow them to cool in the tin for a few minutes, then carefully remove them from the tin. Serve hot with salad or vegetables.

Strawberry Tartlets

Makes
8

These pretty tartlets taste as good as they look! Make them when the fruit is in season for the best flavour or frozen will also work.

Prep
20 mins

Cooking
14 mins

Strawberries

Sieve

Tools

- Rolling pin
- 9cm (3½") fluted cutter
- 12-hole bun tin
- Eight pieces of aluminium foil
- Oven gloves
- Cooling rack

- Small mixing bowl
- Wooden spoon
- Sieve
- Chopping board
- Sharp knife
- Teaspoon
- Small saucepan
- Pastry brush

Ingredients

- 225g (8oz) ready-prepared shortcrust pastry
- 150g (5oz) mascarpone cheese
- ½tsp vanilla extract
- 2tbsp icing sugar
- 175g (6oz) strawberries or other soft fruit
- 4tbsp redcurrant jelly
- 15ml (1tbsp) water

Icing sugar

Bun tin

1 Preheat the oven to 200°C (400°F, gas mark 6). Thinly roll out the pastry, then using a 9cm (3½") fluted cutter, cut out eight circles. Press the pastry circles into a bun tin.

2 Press a piece of scrunched-up foil into each case. Cook for 10 minutes, then remove the foil carefully. Return to the oven for 3–4 minutes. Cool in the tin, then transfer to a cooling rack.

3 To make the filling, place the mascarpone cheese and vanilla extract in a small mixing bowl. Sift over the icing sugar, then beat with a wooden spoon until smooth.

4 Place the strawberries on a chopping board. Remove the green stalks from the strawberries. Then use a sharp knife to cut them in half. (Quarter them if the strawberries are large.)

5 When the pastry cases are completely cool, use a teaspoon to fill them with the mascarpone and vanilla mixture. Arrange the strawberries over the top.

6 Place the redcurrant jelly in a small pan with the water and cook over a low heat, stirring with a wooden spoon until the jelly has dissolved. Brush this over the strawberries.

Apple Crumble

Serves

4-6

Prep

20 mins

Cooking

40 mins

In this twist on a classic dessert, apples are cooked in a rich butterscotch sauce, topped with a crunchy, buttery crumble. Serve with custard or ice cream for the ultimate pudding!

Tools

- Peeler
- Chopping board
- Corer
- Sharp knife
- 900ml (2 pt) ovenproof dish
- Medium saucepan
- Wooden spoon
- Large mixing bowl
- Oven gloves

Corer

Saucepan

Oats

Apples

Ingredients

- 650g (1½lb) cooking apples
- 75g (3oz) light muscovado sugar
- 25g (1oz) butter
- Finely grated zest and juice ½ lemon
- ¼tsp salt
- 100ml (3½floz) water

For the crumble

- 125g (4oz) plain flour
- 75g (3oz) butter (diced)
- 25g (1oz) oats
- 50g (2oz) caster sugar

Butter

Plain flour

1 Preheat the oven to 180°C (350°F, gas mark 4). Using a peeler, peel the apples to remove the skin. Place on a chopping board and use a corer to remove the apple cores.

2 On the chopping board, cut the apples carefully into 2.5cm (1") cube pieces with a sharp knife. Place the pieces in the bottom of an ovenproof dish.

3 Place the sugar, butter, lemon zest and juice and salt in a saucepan with the water. Bring to the boil, stirring occasionally, until the sugar has dissolved and the butter has melted.

Chef's Tip

Don't worry if the butterscotch sauce looks really runny when you pour it over the apples – it will thicken up beautifully in the oven.

4 Pour the butterscotch mixture over the chopped apples in the ovenproof dish and stir with a wooden spoon until he apples are coated evenly in he sauce.

5 Place the flour in a mixing bowl with the diced butter. Using your fingertips, rub in the butter until the mixture looks like rough crumbs. Stir in the oats and the sugar.

6 Spoon the crumble mixture over the top of the apples and bake in the oven on the top shelf for 35–40 minutes until bubbling and golden. Allow to stand for 5 minutes before serving.

Bacon and Egg Tar

When cooked, the cheese in this bacon and egg tart melts to form a lovely crispy top. Delicious hot or cold, the tart tastes especially good with salad.

Serves

6–8

Prep

20 mins

Cooking

50 mins

Eggs

Quiche tin

Ingredients

- 350g (12oz) ready-prepared shortcrust pastry (or see page 99 for a recipe)

For the filling
- 150g (5oz) smoked or unsmoked streaky bacon rashers (chopped)
- 3 medium eggs
- 150ml (¼pt) double cream
- 200ml (7floz) milk
- 1tbsp freshly chopped chives
- Freshly ground black pepper
- 100g (3½oz) Gruyere cheese (grated)

Tools
- Rolling pin
- 23cm (9") loose-bottomed quiche tin
- Fork
- Oven gloves
- Baking paper
- Baking beans or aluminium foil
- Wooden spoon
- Kitchen paper
- Non-stick frying pan
- Kitchen paper
- Large mixing bowl
- Balloon whisk
- Baking tray

Milk

Bacon

Balloon whisk

1 Preheat the oven to 190°C (375°F, gas mark 5). Using a rolling pin, roll out the pastry on a lightly floured surface. Line the loose-bottomed quiche tin with the pastry. Chill for 15 minutes.

2 Prick the base with a fork, line with baking paper and fill with baking beans or scrunched aluminium foil. Bake for 15 minutes. Remove the paper and beans and bake for another 5 minutes.

3 Meanwhile, place the bacon in a non-stick frying pan and cook over a medium heat stirring occasionally until it is crisp. Drain the bacon on kitchen paper.

4 In a large mixing bowl, whisk together the eggs, cream, milk, chives and freshly ground black pepper with a balloon whisk until they are thoroughly combined.

5 Place the pastry case on a baking tray. Scatter the cooked bacon and half the cheese over the pastry base. Pour over the egg mixture, then sprinkle it with the remaining cheese.

6 Place the tray in the oven and bake in the centre for 25–30 minutes until golden and set. Allow to cool for 5 minutes before serving in slices with salad.

Variation

For a cheese and onion tart, omit the bacon. Instead, cook a sliced onion in a little oil until softened and scatter over the base.

Decoration

No cake is complete without some pretty decoration! Whether you use healthy fruit or indulgent icing, here are some top tips for perfect prettiness.

Chef's Tip

Add your liquids, such as water or food colouring, to the icing sugar one drop at a time. You can always add more, but if you add to much it will become too runny.

How to make glacé icing

1 Sift 225g (8oz) icing sugar into a large mixing bowl. You can use your hand or a spoon with the sieve.

2 Gradually stir in 2–3tbsp of hot water. Add a drop of food colouring if you are using it.

How to make buttercream icing

1 Place 75g (3oz) butter in a bowl and beat with a wooden spoon until it has softened.

2 Gradually sift over 175g (6oz) icing sugar. Beat it in with a wooden spoon.

3 Beat in 1–2tbsp milk and/or flavouring until you have a fluffy consistency.

How to make a piping bag

1 Cut out a triangle shape (i.e. half a square) from baking paper. Point the longest side away from you and fold the right hand point over.

2 Fold the left hand point over the cone, bringing all three points together and fold over to secure it in place.

3 Snip off the end with a pair of scissors to create the hole. Put your icing inside the cone and squeeze it out onto the cake. Test it first!

Variations

Here is a selection of cake decorations. They include: sugar strands, sugar flowers, sugar shell chocolate beans and mini-marshmallows.

Glossary

This is the place to find extra information about the baking terms and techniques used in this book.

B

baking blind: weighing down a pastry base with baking beans or foil to stop it from rising during baking.

batch: making or baking things in more than one group, usually if you do not have enough tins or space in the oven.

beat: to stir or mix quickly until smooth, in order to break down or add air.

boil: to heat a liquid such as water to a very hot temperature so that it bubbles and gives off steam.

C

chill: to cool in a refrigerator.

combine: to mix ingredients together.

consistency: how runny or thick a mixture is.

cream: to beat butter and sugar together to add air.

curdle: when the liquid and solid parts of an ingredient or mixture separate. Milk curdles when over-heated and cakes can curdle if the eggs are too cold or added too quickly.

D

dissolve: to melt or liquify a substance (often sugar in water).

drizzle: to pour slowly, in a trickle.

D (dough)

dough: the mixture of flour, water, sugar, salt and yeast (and maybe other ingredients) before it is baked into bread.

E

elastic: a mixture with a stretchy texture.

F

fold: to mix ingredients together gently, to retain as much air in the mixture as possible.

frosting: a topping that is usually a creamy icing.

G

grease: to rub butter onto a baking sheet, tin or tray to prevent the baked item from sticking.

H

hollow: something that is empty. Bread sounds hollow when cooked.

I

individual: a single one, or enough for one person.

K

knead: to press and fold the dough with your hands until it is smooth and stretchy. This distributes the yeast and helps it to rise.

knock back: to deflate risen dough with a gentle punch. This evens out the texture of the bread.

L

level: to make the surface of something the same height.

M

melt: to heat a solid substance until it becomes liquid.

moist: something which is slightly wet.

P

peaks: raised areas that look like the tops of mountains.

preheat: to turn the oven on and heat it to the correct temperature before baking in it.

process: to blend an ingredient or ingredients in a food processor.

Q

quantity: how much of an ingredient you need.

R

rich: strongly flavoured.

ripe: when a fruit is soft and ready to be eaten.

S

sandwich: to stick two sides or halves together, usually with a mixture inbetween.

savoury: something that does not taste sweet.

serrated: the edge of a knife which has 'teeth'.

sift: to use a sieve to strain a dry ingredient and remove lumps.

simmer: to cook over a low heat so the liquid or food is bubbling gently but not boiling.

skewer: a metal or wooden stick with a sharp end.

sprinkle: to scatter a food lightly over another food.

T

texture: the way something feels, e.g. soft, smooth, chunky, moist, etc.

transfer: to move something from one place to another.

trimmings: leftover pieces of dough or pastry from cutting out.

W

well: a dip made in some flour in which to crack an egg or pour liquid.

whisk: to evenly mix ingredients together with a whisk.

Y

yeast: a type of fungus that, when added to flour, water, sugar and salt, ferments and causes the mixture to rise.

Z

zest: the skin of a citrus fruit that has been grated with a grater or zester.

Index

A

almond essence 90
Apple Crumble
118–119
apples 92, 93, 118, 119

B

bacon 120, 121
Bacon and Egg Tart
120–121
**Baked Raspberry
Cheesecake** 96–97
baking blind 99
**Banana and Buttermilk
Cake** 70–71
bananas 70, 94, 95,
108, 109
Banoffee Pie 108–109
Basic Bread 44–45
basil 112, 113
berries 12, 13, 96,
102, 103
biscuits, cookies and
traybakes 8, 9

**Blueberry and Sour
Cream Cake** 78–79
buttercream icing 80
butternut squash 34
butterscotch 118, 119

C

cakes 62, 63
Cake Roll 80–81
cake tins 63
caramel 10, 11, 108, 109
Carrot Cupcakes 68–69
cheese 14, 15, 26, 48, 56,
59, 68, 76, 114, 115, 121
  cream 68, 69
  feta 114
  Parmesan 14, 56
cheesecake 96, 97
**Cheese and Onion
Round** 48–49
Cheesy Oatcakes 26–27
Cheesy Shortbread
14–15
Cherry and Berry Pie
102–103
chocolate 13, 16, 17, 18,

19, 22, 23, 38, 39, 66, 67,
70, 71, 72, 73, 80, 90,
91, 94, 95, 100, 101,
104, 105
  white chocolate 12, 13,
  18, 19, 66
chilli 58
cinnamon 20, 82, 92
**Chocolate and
Cranberry
Cookies** 12–13
Chocolate Tart
104–105
Christmas 30
Chocolate Profiterôles
100–101
Cocoa Mint Meringues
90–91
coconut 36, 86, 87
Coconut Biscuits
36–37
**Chocolate Fudge
Brownies** 38–39
Cornbread 58–59
**Chocolate Fridge
Squares** 16–17
corn flakes 32

courgettes 76
creaming 63
cutting out 9, 25
cranberries 12, 13

D

decoration 30, 31, 40, 41, 122, 123
Double Chocolate Fudge Cake 66–67
dough 42, 43, 51

E

eggs 120, 121

F

fairy cakes 64, 65
Filo and Spinach Tarts 114–115
Flapjacks 32–33
Flatbreads 60–61
focaccia 56, 57
folding in 63
frosting 68, 69, 78, 79

G

garlic 60
ginger 34, 35, 40, 41

Ginger and Pumpkin Slices 34–35
Gingerbread 40–41
golden syrup 37

H

Halloween 30
herbs 26, 56
honey 88, 89
hummous 60
hygiene 7

I

icing 66, 67, 83, 86, 87, 122, 123
  buttercream icing 80, 122
  glacé icing 122
Italian Bread 56–57

J

jam 24, 25, 46, 80, 81, 104
Jam Shapes 24–25

K

kneading 43

L

Lemon Drizzle Cake 74-75
Lemon Meringue 106–107
lemons 74, 75, 106, 107
Lime and Coconut Cupcakes 86–87
lining cake tins 63

M

mango 84
Marble Cake 72–73
marshmallows 18, 19
measuring 9, 37
Melting Moments 22–23
meringues 90, 91, 106, 107
Mini Muffins 94–95
mint 90, 91
mixing 9, 43
Multi-Grain Plait 52–53

N

nuts 16, 17, 38, 70, 71

O

oats 26, 27, 32, 88, 89
Oat and Honey Muffins 88–89
olives 56, 57
onions 48, 121
  spring onions 58, 60
orange 16, 28, 29, 72, 73, 82, 83, 104, 105
Orange and Poppy Seed Muffins 82–83
Orange and Seed Cookies 28–29
oregano 51

P

pastry 98, 99
  filo pastry 99, 114, 115
  choux pastry 99, 100, 101
  puff pastry 99, 102, 103, 112, 113
  shortcrust pastry 99, 104, 105, 106, 107, 116, 117, 120, 121
pineapple 84, 92, 93
piping 23, 123
Pizza Dough 50–51
poppy seeds 82, 83
pumpkin 34, 35

R

Raisin Biscuits 20–21
raspberries 96, 97
rising 43
Rocky Road Cookies 18–19
rolling 9, 99
rolls 45
rosemary 26, 56, 60

S

safe baking 6
salads 26, 48, 58, 112
Savoury Muffins 76–77
sunflower seeds 28, 29
Scones 46–47
shaping 43
Simple Sponge Cake 64–65
soups 48, 58
sour cream 78, 79
spinach 76, 114, 115
sponge cakes 64, 65, 74, 75, 80, 81
Star Biscuits 30–31
Sticky Fruit Buns 54–55
storage 9
Strawberry Tartlets 116–117
strawberries 116, 117
sweetcorn 58

T

temperature 63
testing a cake 63
Toffee Squares 10–11
Tomato and Basil Tart 112–113
tomatoes 56, 57, 112, 113
Tropical Fruit Cake 84–85

U

Upside-down Apple Cake 92–93

V

Valentine's Day 19, 30
vanilla essence 87, 90

Y

yeast 43
yoghurt 89